INTEGRATION AND COMMUNITY BUILDING IN EASTERN EUROPE

INTEGRATION AND COMMUNITY BUILDING IN EASTERN EUROPE

Jan F. Triska, series editor

The German Democratic Republic
Arthur M. Hanhardt, Jr.

The Polish People's Republic
James F. Morrison

The Development of Socialist Yugoslavia
M. George Zaninovich

The People's Republic of Albania
Nicholas C. Pano

The Czechoslovak Socialist Republic
Zdenek Suda

The Socialist Republic of Rumania
Stephen Fischer-Galati

THE
Socialist
Republic of
Rumania

STEPHEN FISCHER-GALATI

THE JOHNS HOPKINS PRESS

Baltimore

FOREWORD

This monograph on the Socialist Republic of Rumania by Professor Stephen Fischer-Galati is an empirical analysis and a case study of the relations Rumania has had with the other states ruled by communist parties. As in the other studies in this series—on the U.S.S.R., Communist China, North Korea, Outer Mongolia, and so on*—the focus here is on Rumania as a political unit interacting with the other communist party states. It is not a single descriptive study of a communist ruled country, the Socialist Republic of Rumania; instead, it is a study of Rumania as a unit *within* the communist party-state system, a part of a collective, systematic intellectual effort to assess empirically the scope, rate, and direction of integration among the states ruled by communist parties. This is why Professor Fischer-Galati's focus of attention is that behavior and data of Rumania relevant to integration and community formation with its neighbors and friends in the East.

* The first four monographs in this series were published in the Hoover Institution Studies Series, *Integration and Community Building Among the Fourteen Communist Party-States*: Glenn D. Paige, *The Korean People's Democratic Republic*; Robert A. Rupen, *The Mongolian People's Republic*; Vernon V. Aspaturian, *The Soviet Union in the World Communist System*; Dennis J. Doolin and Robert C. North, *The Chinese People's Republic* (all 1966).

Is Rumania slated to follow the tragic fate of Czechoslovakia? Rumania's more recent relations with the other socialist states, in particular with the Soviet Union, have been of the maverick kind. At times Rumania has behaved, in spite of its geographic location, as if it were indeed an independent, uncommitted state. "The basic factor in evaluating the current, and prognosticating the future, Rumanian policies toward integration and community building [in Eastern Europe]," writes Professor Fischer-Galati, "remains that of irreconcilability of the fundamental political conflict with the Soviet Union. A meaningful reconciliation appears unlikely so long as the present Rumanian and Russian ruling élites remain in power. So long as that situation persists, anything but *pro forma* reintegration of Rumania into the Soviet bloc is excluded. This is not to say that integration would be detrimental to Rumania were it possible to achieve it under terms safeguarding the Rumanian Party's vital political interests. In the absence of such safeguards, Rumania's 'independent course' is likely to be pursued, albeit with greater caution and finesse. Should Ceausescu be able to walk the tight-rope successfully, his regime would be assured of ever greater popular support; his 'socialist nationalist' goals may, however, prove elusive."

On the other hand, Rumania's party leadership has introduced no startling innovations at home which would match its quasi-independent relations with the socialist countries as yet. Unlike Czechoslovakia, Rumania, while effectively pressing for greater freedom of maneuver for itself in Eastern Europe, essentially toes the old line at home. This seems to be perceived by its socialist neighbors as the lesser of two evils. In addition, of course, Rumania on the Black Sea does not pose the kind of "threat to national security of the

U.S.S.R.," as Mr. Kosygin put it, that West Germany's neighbor, Czechoslovakia, did.

Like the other authors in this series, Stephen Fischer-Galati uses the concept of integration to describe such cooperative behavior where coordination—systems of information and adjustment of courses of action—is the efficient basis for joint action leading to a common goal. If all relevant units of the system are so involved, he speaks of integrated behavior; if most are involved, he speaks of extensive integration; and so on. A system may thus be integrated or not in a variety of ways, depending on the number and effectiveness of involved units.

In addition, a system may be integrated at the top level of authority, or it may be integrated on subordinate levels. The authority, furthermore, may be based essentially on coercion, or it may stem essentially from consensus. Which of these variants is more conducive to integrated behavior? Under what circumstances, when, and to what ends?

Stephen Fischer-Galati systematically tries to answer these questions by examining closely the data he has painstakingly collected. He discusses integration of Rumania into the communist party states both as a *condition* in which he found the country and as a *process*—Rumania becoming integrated into the system.

Like the other authors in the series, Professor Fischer-Galati analyzes first the data potentially conducive to integration—in this case, Rumania's historical legacy, ecological-physical factors, demographic structure, social system, degree of autonomy, and dependence upon other states. This is the pre-entry period of Rumania—the analytical description of Rumania before it became a communist party state. The entry and postentry years are broken down into four distinct periods: intensive socialist development, the post-Stalin era, the thaw, and the present stage. For each of these periods the author examines various elements of the Rumanian communist-based society (e.g., the belief system, the political system, etc.) and attempts to detect salient changes in them.

This series is an intellectual product of many creative minds. In addition to the authors of the individual monographs—in this case, Professor Stephen Fischer-Galati—I would like to thank Professor David D. Finley of Stanford University and Colorado College for his original contribution and assistance.

JAN F. TRISKA

Institute of Political Studies
Stanford University

The Socialist Republic of Rumania
Republica Socialista Romania

Area: 92,800 square miles
Population: 19,500,000 (1968 est.)
Communist Party membership: 1,600,000 (1968 est.)

Major cities:	Population:
Bucuresti (capital)	1,511,390
Brasov	263,200
Cluj	222,650
Constanta	199,360
Iasi	194,840
Timisoara	193,040
Ploiesti	190,690

Population distribution: 37% urban, 63% rural

Birth rate: 14.3 per 1,000 (1966)
Death rate: 8.2 per 1,000 (1966)

Total school enrollment: 4,170,877 (1966/67)
Illiteracy rate (9 years and older): nil (1968 est.)
Higher education enrollment: 137,677 (1966/67)
Daily newspapers combined daily circulation: 2,727,611 (1966)
Cinemas: 6,467 (1966)
Radio receivers: 2,051,000 (1966)
Public libraries: 11,036 (1966)
Number of physicians: 28,900 (1966)

Road network: 76,598 km. (1966)
Railroad network: 11,007 km. (1966)
National income by sector (1966):
Industry, 49.7%; building, 8%; agriculture and forestry, 29.7%; transport and telecommunications, 4.1%; trade, 6%; other branches, 2.5%

Principal natural resources: Oil, coal, copper, gold, uranium, timber, bauxite, salt, water power

Principal products: Meat, bread grains, fodder, vegetables, lumber, petroleum products, production machinery and equipment

Foreign trade (1966):
Exports:	$593,075,000
Imports:	$606,608,333
Total:	$1,199,683,333

Principal trading partners: U.S.S.R., West Germany, Czechoslovakia, East Germany, Italy, France, England
Currency: $1 = 12 lei   Metric system

CONTENTS

The Socialist Republic of Rumania

INTRODUCTION

The current Rumanian position in international affairs is complex, and replete with contradictions and dilemmas. Rumania is a communist state, interested in the unity of the socialist camp; at the same time it seeks consolidation and expansion of relations with the nations outside the socialist camp, on the basis of equality and mutual advantage.

This international position was reached by necessity rather than by choice. In Stalin's time, Rumania's strength was based as much on Russian support as on Rumanian Stalinism, and the country could ill afford meaningful relations with the West until the threat to the Rumanian Stalinists' political survival became greater from the East than from the West. Since 1954, when international Khrushchevism sought the eradication of Rumanian Stalinism and of its leaders, Gheorghiu-Dej and his associates and followers have thought in terms of seeking leverage from the West as well as from fellow nationalist Stalinists in the East. To legitimize their power, at the Party and state levels, they have also claimed the historic legacies of the Rumanian communist movement and of Greater Rumania and sought recognition of the validity of their claims from the Rumanian people and the international community as a whole.

The concurrent reliance on Western economic support and on Chinese political support to counter economic and political pressures from Russia ensured the survival of the Rumanian nationalist-Stalinist leadership. Rumania then strengthened its independence and, by 1964, had become a "neutral" force in the international communist movement and a potential intermediary in East-West relations. The gradual deterioration of Sino-Rumanian relations, subsequent to Bucharest's refusal fully to endorse Chinese positions, and the growing isolation of China from the international communist movement in general, has forced ever greater reliance on the West.

Even before the walkout from the Budapest Conference of February, 1968, Rumania was assuming the position of a neutral state, albeit communist, not only within the socialist camp but within the international community as a whole. The role of the "honest broker" in all international disputes—between East and West, between the Soviet bloc and the Chinese, between the *tiers monde* and the committed—is actively sought by Bucharest.

This role has strongly affected the relationships between Rumania and fellow communist party states, and the potential and actual integration and community building among these states, which are discussed in the present monograph. Whether the pursuit of this course will still be possible after the Soviet invasion of Czechoslovakia and the resulting threat to Rumania's own independence is one of the major questions facing the international community.

1: RUMANIA IN THE PRE-ENTRY PERIOD

Historical Legacy

U p to the end of World War II, Rumania was generally regarded as a backward, corrupt, and disreputable Balkan state. Tsar Nicholas II's only *bon mot*, "Rumania is not a nationality but a profession," epitomized the impression of those familiar with Rumanian politics in the twentieth century.[1]

An objective appraisal of this diagnosis, in the light of the historic perspective, would not necessarily question its accuracy but would offer explanations for it. The history of Rumania has been one of unrealized expectations. Since its inception in the Roman era Rumania has had a history of dissolution, division, and struggle for survival. The historic antecedents of the second century A.D., when the territory inhabited by the future Rumanians included virtually all lands comprising Rumania today, are still invoked by Rumanian historians and statesmen as the basis for a correct interpretation of the country's historic evolu-

[1] Excellent historical treatises are Constantin C. Giurescu, *Istoria Romanilor* ("History of the Rumanians") (Bucharest, 1940–44) and Nicolae Iorga, *Istoria Romanilor* ("History of the Rumanians") (Bucharest, 1936–39). The best history of the Rumanians in English is by R. W. Seton-Watson, *A History of the Roumanians* (Cambridge, 1934).

3

tion. The restoration of that golden age of power, wealth, and grandeur—albeit in contemporary garb—has been the ostensible goal of Rumanian leaders since the dissolution of the Daco-Roman state began in the third century. That dissolution was complete some time before the founding of the principal component provinces of the Rumanian state of the future, Wallachia and Moldavia, around 1300. By that time the important region of Transylvania was part of Hungary, and Wallachia and Moldavia themselves had close ties with the Hungarian kingdom. The division of the three major parts of what is now Rumania was deepened and prolonged by the Turkish conquest of the Balkans and the Turkish advance into East Central Europe which began in the fourteenth century, and by the contemporary expansion of Habsburg power in the same area. Wallachia and Moldavia became vassal states of the Ottoman Empire, while Transylvania fell first under Ottoman and later under Habsburg domination. The historically relevant aspects of political and socioeconomic life were, in Moldavia and Wallachia, serfdom and corruption; in Transylvania, serfdom and denationalization.

The oppression of the peasantry was more cruel in Wallachia and Moldavia because the Turks' exactions increased severely during the decline of the Ottoman Empire after the middle of the sixteenth century. But the demands of the Turks, and of the Greeks, who were the main executors of Turkish will in the Rumanian provinces, do not account exclusively for the prevalent destitution and deprivation. The Rumanian feudal aristocracy and ruling princes themselves collaborated with the Turks and their agents to maintain their rights and privileges, and in the process resorted to the same methods of fiscal evasion, bribery, and extortion, to the very mores and practices that characterized the officials of the Ottoman Empire. Fortunately for all concerned, the enormous agricultural resources of the Rumanian provinces assured the enrichment of all oligarchies and at least the marginal survival of the peasant.

The problems were somewhat different in Transylvania, where the exploitation of the peasant masses was not connected with a Rumanian feudal aristocracy or with Turkish masters. There the majority of the peasantry was Rumanian and the feudal lords were Hungarian. The Rumanian serfs in Transylvania enjoyed a much higher standard of living than those in Moldavia and Wallachia; such opposition as was expressed against the socioeconomic and political order was based on the denial of the Rumanians' political existence by the dominant nationalities—the Hungarian, Saxon, and Szekler. The absence of social mobility for the few Rumanian intellectuals, merchants, and landowners led, in the eighteenth century, to the voicing of political demands by this Rumanian élite, who sought the recognition of the Rumanian nation as a political entity in the province. By the early nineteenth century, demands for political rights, even political autonomy, were proposed separately but not independently by leaders in all Rumanian provinces—Transylvania, Wallachia, and Moldavia—but socioeconomic reform for the masses was at best an insignificant aspect of the programs of the politically conscious.

As a consequence, at least in Moldavia and Wallachia, political activity was restricted to the problems of agrarian-feudal societies and reflected the interests of the feudal élite. Throughout most of the nineteenth century these interests were equated with governance by a Rumanian aristocratic oligarchy, without inter-

5

ference by the Turkish suzerain or the overprotective
and growingly imperialistic Russian empire. The divisive issue in Wallachian and Moldavian political
life was whether the modernizing aristocracy, exposed
to French influences, should lead the struggle for independence or whether that task should be entrusted
to the conservative feudal aristocracy, closely tied to
conservative Russia. The conflict was at least temporarily resolved in 1859 when the two Rumanian provinces were united into an autonomous Rumania ruled
by the "liberal" elements of the aristocratic champions
of independence. But the modernizers themselves had
a narrow concept of modernization: they opposed, almost as ardently as the conservatives, the breaking up
of the village, which would have freed the manpower
required for the exploitation of Rumania's nonagri-
cultural riches. The politics of "neo-serfdom"—as
characterized by a leading critic of pre-World War I
Rumania—prevailed even after the establishment of
the independent state, the Old Kingdom, in 1878, and
the development of a primitive Rumanian industry
in the late nineteenth and early twentieth centuries.
In an unsuccessful effort to contain peasant discontent (there was a major peasant revolt in 1907), the
rulers of Rumania substituted nationalism for social
reform as the political panacea for all inhabitants. The
union of all Rumanians, whether inhabiting Hungarian Transylvania, Austrian Bukovina, Russian Bessarabia, or the Turkish Dobrudja, became the political
raison d'être of "liberals" and "conservatives" as
World War I approached.

These narrow political views and broad territorial
aspirations were only partly shared by the Rumanians
of Transylvania, where political activity was directed
toward the establishment of a viable and unitary Ru-

manian nation. From the middle of the nineteenth century the goal of all Rumanians, whether politically conscious intellectuals and bourgeoisie or peasantry, was the gaining of political equality with the privileged nations—Magyar, Szekler, or Saxon—and the modernization of Rumanian society. Rejection of the Rumanians' national aspirations by the Austro-Hungarian political oligarchy did not prevent the gradual evolution of an affluent middle class, an organized industrial labor force, and a reasonably prosperous peasantry—all accepting the political leadership of an intellectual-bourgeois coalition, the Transylvanian National Party. As the intransigence of the dominant nations increased in the early twentieth century, the Transylvanians regarded national unification into a Greater Rumania with favor, but not at the cost of sacrificing the nonpolitical gains realized under Austro-Hungarian rule. And the same desires and reservations were entertained by the Rumanians in other parts of the Austro-Hungarian state, including Bukovina, and even by those in Bessarabia as World War I ended the empire of the Habsburgs and the tsars and made the creation of a Greater Rumanian state, focusing on the only victorious component, the Old Kingdom, an inevitable political reality.

Greater Rumania did not prove viable for a variety of reasons.[2] Politically, it was threatened from its inception with revisionistic claims by Hungary, Bulgaria, and Russia for territories acquired by Rumania in the process of integration. The seriousness of these demands could be discounted in the twenties, but they were used by the political leaders of the Old Kingdom

[2] The most authoritative study of Greater Rumania is by Henry L. Roberts, *Rumania: Political Problems of an Agrarian State* (New Haven, 1951).

as justification for retaining political power as defenders of Rumania's territorial integrity and national interest. The defense of the country by its creators was also directed against "internal enemies" such as national minorities, "communists" and their sympathizers, and all other politically conscious or organized segments of the population that were seeking a more equitable distribution of political power and a greater role in the modernization of the state. Refusal to accept the party system as an instrument of political action and expression led first to political paternalism by the Bucharest oligarchy headed by the Bratianu family, and, in the thirties, to royal authoritarianism, culmination in the establishment of a royal dictatorship under King Carol II in 1938. The political conflict in the years between the world wars focused on agrarian problems and the role of the peasantry in Greater Rumania. The major agrarian reform, precipitated by the Bolshevik Revolution and enacted in the Old Kingdom at the end of the war, together with the reconfirmation of the rights of the peasantry, could have led to the gaining of political power by the peasantry through peasant parties. That disaster was averted, with a resulting isolation of the villages, continuing substitution of nationalism for socioeconomic and political reform, and consolidation of the power of the political establishment. That establishment, consisting before the war of the "liberal" and "conservative" parties, and after the war of the Wallachian and Moldavian middle class and conservative intellectuals, fought for the maintenance of the status quo. The development of the country's vast economic resources was neglected. Industrialization proceeded slowly, frequently with inadequate capital. Social welfare and education fared badly. The mechanization of agriculture was nominal. Nevertheless, the tremendous natural wealth in agricultural products, petroleum, and minerals, combined with a cheap labor force, permitted the development of an industrial base and the maintenance of relative prosperity and stability at least until the Great Depression.

The depression ushered in a period of grave difficulties for Rumania, not all economic. In fact, the economic problems per se had only a marginal effect on the underdeveloped agrarian economy and the slowly developing industry. The problems faced by the country were political, related to the rise of Hitler's Germany, the consolidation of the Stalinist order in Russia, and the weakening of the West. In the thirties the Germans became Rumania's principal customers and in the process extended their sphere of economic and political influence into the country. This led, on the one hand, to acceleration of industrial development and general economic growth and, on the other, to the strengthening of Rumanian fascism. Rumanian fascism, of a populist–anti-Semitic variety, antedated Hitler's. Organized in the Iron Guard, it gained momentum in the thirties, seeking and securing the support of the disgruntled peasantry for a national Christian crusade against the existing political establishment, the city, and the Jew, and for redistributing the national wealth to the masses. That momentum grew steadily, with German financial and moral support, until the party system was abolished in 1938 by King Carol II. The strength of the fascists was the decisive factor in the establishment of the royal dictatorship. But Carol acted also in the defense of the country against potential aggression by the revisionist Soviet Union, Nazi Germany, and the Axis' revisionist allies, Hungary and Bulgaria.

The stability ensured by dictatorship was precarious and short-lived. Greater Rumania crumbled in 1940 under the extreme pressures generated by foreign revisionists and Rumanian fascists. The Soviet Union, following the Molotov-Ribbentrop agreement, seized Bessarabia and northern Bukovina. The Hungarians and Bulgarians, with German support, annexed northern Transylvania and southern Dobrudja. The Rumanian fascists, blaming the King for dismemberment of the country, forced his abdication and assumed power as the German armies were occupying Rumania as a base for the forthcoming conflict with the U.S.S.R. A new dictatorship, under General Ion Antonescu, replaced that of King Carol and pursued a policy of national unification for the purpose of recovering the territories lost to Russia and fighting a national Christian crusade against communism. The war against the Soviet Union began in June, 1941, and ended in August, 1944, when the Rumanians abandoned Antonescu and Nazi Germany as the Red Army neared Bucharest.

Throughout her history, Rumania has displayed a basic reluctance toward integration with other states, particularly the present party states of the communist system.[3] The historic Rumanian provinces—Moldavia and Wallachia—jealously guarding the modicum of autonomy bestowed upon them by the Turks, avoided associations with the future nation states of Bulgaria or Serbia, for example, as long as these areas were Turkish pashaliks, for fear of jeopardizing their own

[3] These problems are considered in Stephen Fischer-Galati, "The Rumanians and the Habsburg Monarchy," *Austrian History Yearbook*, III, part II (1967), 430–49, and in Andrei Otetea, "The Rumanians and the Disintegration of the Habsburg Monarchy," *ibid.*, pp. 450–76.

relatively privileged position. Possible integration with other nations—enemies of the Ottoman Empire—was also resisted in the same spirit. Austrian attempts to transform Wallachia into a dependency were as strenuously opposed in the eighteenth century as were earlier Polish attempts at incorporation of Moldavia into the Polish kingdom. In the nineteenth and early twentieth centuries Rumanian goals were the opposite of integration: first the United Principalities of Moldavia and Wallachia, then the Old Kingdom, were active promoters of the disintegration of the Habsburg Empire and a main force in precipitating the ultimate dissolution of that empire as well as of the Ottoman. The history of Wallachia and Moldavia does not record enthusiasm for integration into the empire of the Russian tsars, particularly after Russia's imperialistic intentions became evident in the eighteenth century. The Rumanians were singularly opposed to Panslavism and to their inclusion by the Russians among those to be liberated from foreign oppressors.

The other provinces that were to become components of Greater Rumania at the end of World War I showed no greater interest in integration than the Old Kingdom itself. Transylvania, Bukovina, and Bessarabia were thorns in the flesh of the Habsburg and Romanov emperors for nearly one hundred and fifty years before World War I, and then of Greater Rumania. Even the Dobrudja, though more pliable than the other constituent provinces of Greater Rumania, showed no propensity toward integration. Most significantly, the divisive forces generated by particularism in these provinces prevented their effective integration into a United Rumania after 1918. What was the relative importance of these internally divisive forces in impeding integration then and now? May it not be argued that external factors overshadowed domestic considerations after the establishment of the independent Rumanian state in 1878 and of Greater Rumania at the end of World War I? Indeed, how relevant is the historic legacy in the formulation and implementation of policies favoring or opposing integration with other states?

Economic Structure

Pre-communist Rumania was an underdeveloped agrarian country, with the notable exception of its industrial exploitation of petroleum and its development, on a modest scale, of corollary industries.[4] The production of cereals—principally wheat and maize—was high by East European standards. Between 1921 and 1925, for instance, the average yearly production of these crops amounted to 24,377,000 and 35,613,000 quintals (1 quintal = 220 lbs.). By 1938 these figures were 49,124,000 and 52,231,000, respectively. By contrast, the production from food-processing and industrial plants was nominal. Cereals and wood constituted the bulk of Rumania's export trade: in 1925, 25 per cent and 23 per cent, respectively; in 1938, 25 per cent and 11 per cent. Animal products represented only a small fraction of the export trade (about 10 per cent in 1938), the balance consisting almost entirely of petroleum (40 per cent of the total trade in the 1930's).

Rumania's oil deposits, the second largest in Europe, have been exploited systematically since the middle of the nineteenth century. Modernization of

[4] Valuable data on Rumania's economic structure and development are contained in Joseph S. Roucek, *Contemporary Roumania and Her Problems* (Stanford, 1932), pp. 247–353.

equipment and extractive techniques occurred only after World War I, with dramatic increases in output. Thus in 1921 crude oil production amounted to only 1,168,000 tons; it reached 8,703,000 in 1936, and declined, because of decreased export requirements, to 6,225,000 on the eve of World War II. It is characteristic of the country's underdeveloped industrial capacity that until Rumania became communist, crude oil rather than petroleum derivates were exported. In terms of value of exports, those derived from petroleum amounted to over 40 per cent of the total Rumanian export trade in the nineteen thirties.

Industrial production not related to petroleum output was marginal in the thirties. The most significant area of development was the food industry: 974 industrial establishments (with more than 20 employees) out of a total of 3,767 in the country as a whole were devoted to food production in 1938. The total investment of capital in the food industry was 10.7 billion lei ($25,000,000 at the free market rate of exchange) —approximately 20 per cent of the total capital invested in Rumanian industry in 1938. The chemical, metallurgic, textile, and wood industries were the next most developed, but the total investment of capital in all these together amounted to a mere 31 billion lei. Significantly, the total personnel in all Rumanian industry on the eve of World War II was just under 300,000, and the total of the salaries paid to those workers was 8.3 billion lei. Rumanian industrial production, except for agricultural products and petroleum, was insufficient to meet even the modest requirements of the country's inhabitants.

Thus before World War II Rumania produced and exported raw materials and imported almost exclusively finished goods. Between 1929 and 1938 over 80 per cent of the total imports were finished goods. Most of the lucrative trade was with West European countries, particularly Germany, which was normal considering the overabundance of agricultural products in Eastern Europe and the general lack of industrial development in that area. These factors account also for the absence of a tradition of regional economic cooperation and, in the current perspective, for the continuing Rumanian opposition to Russian schemes for economic integration of the bloc under COMECON (Council for Mutual Economic Aid).

Ecological-physical Factors

Consideration of relevant ecological-physical features as factors for or against integration yields contradictory results. The contiguous open borders with Russia, Bulgaria, and Serbia, for example, could have facilitated integration with these present members of the communist state system. In reality, however, the opposite was the case, since the very concept of integration beyond that of political alignments was unknown to the essentially feudal Old Kingdom. Nationalism in its primitive forms was clearly the determining factor in international relations, as the prewar alliances testify. Proximity to Russia was regarded as a handicap in the attainment of the national goal of a Greater Rumania; and the other neighboring states—Serbia, Bulgaria, and Hungary—either entertained rival claims to those of the Rumanians or were the would-be victims of Bucharest's territorial ambitions in Rumanian-inhabited areas. Ecological-physical factors should also have favored closer integration efforts by Greater Rumania. The acquisition of Transylvania and other areas rich in natural resources should have facilitated economic cooperation at least with Hungary and Yugoslavia, yet such opportunities were again subordinated to political considerations, and obstacles were raised by Hungarian irredentists, German imperialists, and Russian communists. The maintenance of the territorial gains realized at the end of World War I against claims by neighboring countries transcended all other factors.

There is no evidence that domestic ecological-physical factors affected the official Rumanian attitude toward international cooperation. Localism and provincialism, aggravated by the geographic isolation of certain communities and even provinces, were inconsequential to Bucharest.

Demographic Structure

The country's demographic structure, on the other hand, explains some of the most obvious difficulties related to international cooperation.[5] The size of the population nearly quadrupled between 1878 and 1918, increasing from 4,500,000 to nearly 18,000,000. By 1941, subsequent to the loss of northern Transylvania, southern Dobrudja, Bessarabia, and northern Bukovina, Rumania's population fell to 13,500,000. At the end of World War II, through restoration of the Transylvanian territories lost in 1940, the population again rose to approximately 16,000,000. The urban-rural distribution remained relatively constant between 1878 and 1945, fluctuating between 15 and 85 per cent and

[5] A concise survey of the relevant demographic factors is contained in Fred S. Pisky, "The People," in *Romania,* ed. Stephen Fischer-Galati (New York, 1957), pp. 35–58. See also Central Statistical Board, *Statistical Pocket Book of the Socialist Republic of Romania, 1967* (Bucharest, 1967), pp. 25–31.

23 and 77 per cent on the respective dates. In 1930 the proportion was 20 to 80 per cent. It is noteworthy that only five towns in Greater Rumania had more than 100,000 inhabitants at any given time before the establishment of the communist regime—Bucharest, Cluj, Timisoara, Ploesti, and Iasi. Each had a population of approximately 100,000, except Bucharest, whose size varied between 600,000 inhabitants in 1918 and 1,000,000 in 1945. It is also remarkable that of the 13,500 towns and communes in Rumania at the end of World War II, fewer than 200 had a population in excess of 5,000, and nearly 10,000 had less than 1,000 inhabitants.

Ethnic and Language Groups

The ethnic composition of the population remained fairly constant between 1918 and 1945, except for major fluctuations in the German and Jewish groups. The overwhelming majority were Rumanians (80 to 85 per cent); the largest minorities were the Hungarians (10 per cent), the Germans (5 per cent until the end of World War II and 2 per cent after their resettlement), and the Jews (1 per cent at the end of World War II, but about 8 per cent in the interwar period). The rest of the minorities, including Gypsies, Serbs, and Croats, Russians, Bulgarians, Turks, Poles, Tartars, Albanians, and others, comprised approximately 2 per cent of the total population. The linguistic divisions followed those of the ethnic cultures, except for the Jewish population which, in most instances, spoke Rumanian.

Religious Groups

The population of Rumania has always been overwhelmingly Greek Orthodox. In 1938 the Orthodox Church had 13,000,000 adherents as compared with the 1,400,000 Uniates (Greek Catholics), 1,275,000 Roman Catholics, 700,000 Calvinists, 750,000 Jews, and 400,000 Lutherans. Following the territorial readjustments at the end of World War II, these figures varied slightly in accordance with the relocation of the German population, Jewish emigration, and war losses. Nevertheless, nearly 80 per cent of the population belonged to the Greek Orthodox faith, whereas the Roman Catholic membership declined by approximately 275,000, the Calvinist by 125,000, the Lutheran by 150,000, and, more significantly, the Jewish by 500,000.

Belief System and Social System

Demographic factors, including the weighty question of illiteracy, become important in any consideration of the belief and social systems of Rumania. The percentage of illiteracy in the Old Kingdom, which was inhabited almost exclusively by Rumanians of the Orthodox faith, had declined from 78 per cent in 1900 to approximately 60 per cent at the time of the establishment of Greater Rumania. In Transylvania and the Banat illiteracy amounted to approximately 40 per cent in 1918 and was confined primarily to the Rumanian population. Incorporation of these regions into Greater Rumania further increased the gulf between the Rumanian masses on the one hand and the Rumanian aristocracy, bourgeoisie, intellectuals, and non-

Rumanian population on the other. The comparative reduction of illiteracy to a total of 38 per cent in 1930 to 23 per cent in 1948 has not altered this gulf, which, more than other internally generated factors, has affected the integration potential, if not the integration policies, of Greater Rumania.

Basic Values and Goal Values, Cultural Orientation, and Religion

The official "national" Rumanian goals prior to the establishment of the communist regime may be defined as the attainment of a Greater Rumania, and subsequent to that achievement, the preservation of the Greater Rumanian state. These goals, however, represented the lowest common denominator of the aims of the various elements and groups of the heterogeneous population and were devised largely as substitutes for satisfaction of basic socioeconomic and political desiderata. Before the establishment of the Greater Rumanian state, the conflict between the official goal and the desires of the masses was self-evident. In the compact Old Kingdom, the boyar dominated, landlord oligarchy was determined to seek national aggrandizement as a panacea for all problems. The goals of this "neo-feudal" order conflicted directly with the basic goal of the peasantry—individual ownership of land subsequent to a radical land reform. Mass identification with the nationalistic policies of the Rumanian government was minimal; by exploiting religious prejudices, however, the ruling groups were able to develop anti-Semitism as a domestic nationalist tradition. The Jew, traditional moneylender and estate manager for the frequently absent landlord class, was depicted by priest and teacher alike as the exploiter, and therefore the enemy, of the Rumanian peasant. While the influence of such arguments on the masses was not as great as expected, it nevertheless developed a sense of national consciousness at least among the younger members of the peasantry. The identification of rural prejudices with the professed national aim of the oligarchy did not eliminate the fundamental conflict between the goals of the masses and the ruling class, nor did the superficially pro-Western cultural orientation of the aristocracy and bourgeoisie alter the realities of the goal conflict. The predominantly pro-French cultural ties stressed the "Latin" aspects of both Rumania and France. This common heritage was interpreted as a mandate for irredentism rather than for social reform in the French manner. It militated against international cooperation with neighboring states, all of which were irredentist as well as non-Latin.[6]

The complex goals of the various ethnic, religious, and socioeconomic groups of Greater Rumania, and the conflict between them and the official "national goal" of maintenance of the Greater Rumanian state are, however, far more relevant to the basic problems raised by this paper. The multinationalization of Rumania deepened the contradictions between the aims of the ruling class and those of the masses, insofar as most non-Rumanian elements were opposed to that very goal. A majority of the Hungarians of Transylvania and the Banat, for instance, favored Rumania's

[6] Scholarly analyses of these problems are contained in Roberts, *Rumania,* pp. 3 ff.; Eugen Weber, "Romania," in *The European Right: A Historical Profile,* eds. Hans Rogger and Eugen Weber (Berkeley, 1966), pp. 501 ff.; Stephen Fischer-Galati, *The New Rumania: From People's Democracy to Socialist Republic* (Cambridge, Mass., 1967), pp. 1 ff.

"disintegration" and the incorporation of these provinces within a reconstituted Hungary. This counter-irredentism was also manifest among the Bulgarians of southern Dobrudja and, to a considerable extent, among the Transylvanian Germans following Hitler's rise to power. Furthermore, the socioeconomic goals and cultural orientation of the Hungarians and Germans was at variance with that of the Rumanians. This was less true of the peasant groups, who nevertheless regarded themselves as superior to their Rumanian peers, than of the bourgeoisie inhabiting the *Sieben Bürgen*. The members of the middle class regarded themselves as heirs to and exponents of a Hungarian or German culture, with strongly anti-French overtones and with definite contempt for the parvenu, neo-Latin Rumanians. These sentiments, reflecting general dissatisfaction with Rumanian rule, were encouraged by the Catholic and Protestant churches, thereby increasing the friction between Bucharest and the non-Rumanian Transylvanians.

The belief system of the minority groups in other parts of pre-communist Rumania is of little importance to us here; no clearly defined goals, cultural orientation, or religious conflicts need to be singled out. Although they did not oppose the regime directly, none of the minority groups endorsed the official national goal. More significantly, the goals of the Rumanian masses remained in conflict with those of the ruling classes; the official doctrines in domestic and foreign affairs enjoyed only limited acceptance by the majority of the inhabitants of Greater Rumania.

It is evident that the prewar ruling oligarchy, whose power before the agrarian reform of 1918–21 had rested on control of the land as well as of the peasant, was forced by circumstances to alter its goals; the economic base of the ruling class had to be readjusted. Although land ownership still constituted a significant part of the rulers' wealth, participation in industrial and financial ventures assumed greater importance. Thus, employment in the state or private bureaucracy, preferably as front men for foreign and Jewish capitalists, or as members of the diplomatic corps, was the ultimate goal of the postwar ruling élite. These aims and ambitions came into direct conflict not only with those of the non-Rumanian bourgeoisie but also with those of the rising groups of second-generation Rumanian peasants, whose social and political mobility was limited by the pre-empting of the key political and economic positions by the former landlord class and their descendants. As compromises were reached with ethnic Rumanians of the Old Kingdom and Transylvania, the co-opted elements assumed the attitudes and goals of their benefactors.

The preservation of privileges and of Greater Rumania itself were the paramount goals of the entire ruling class. In order to maintain its position, that class encouraged, or at least condoned, both domestic and foreign-oriented nationalistic manifestations, including chauvinism and anti-Semitism at home, and counter-irredentism in relations with Rumania's neighbors. In justification and defense of Greater Rumania, this group emphasized the country's Latin roots and relied on French political protection. These considerations transcended the realities of domestic and international pressures and, given the superficiality of the élite's aims, did not encourage economic integration or inter-Balkan cooperation against common external enemies. Rumania was officially depicted as the tradi-

21

tional friend of France in the East, as a country culturally superior to its Balkan neighbors and to the Soviet Union, and as a Latin oasis in southeastern Europe. Bucharest was proudly proclaimed the Paris of the East, and international cooperation was possible only with other superior or like-minded East European nations, particularly Czechoslovakia and Poland. Countries like Bulgaria and Albania were held in contempt; Hungary, a revisionist nation, was treated with nationalistic hatred; Yugoslavia, though not highly esteemed, was nevertheless tolerated for reasons of political security.

Degree of Integration of Rumania
with Other Systems

The prevalence of such attitudes meant that the crises of the interwar years, although understood, were not subject to rational solutions. French protection and reliance on the Little Entente were regarded as adequate barriers against pressures exerted by Communist Russia and Nazi Germany. Neither compromise nor cooperation with the Soviet Union were accepted, because of the dual threats of communism and revisionism. Cooperation with Hitler's Germany could be rationalized in terms of German anticommunism, anti-Semitism, and, until 1940, neutrality toward Hungarian and Bulgarian revisionism. It is noteworthy that the positive economic advantages offered by Germany to an economically distraught Rumania during the depression years were not regarded as an excuse or justification for cooperation.

The integration potential of Greater Rumania was further diminished by the social, economic, and political pressures generated by an unstable social system.[7] As in all East European countries, there was little correlation between the aspirations of the masses and official policies. Political decisions were seldom made at the polls (where intimidation, bribery, and fraud were the rule), or in Parliament, even before the abolition of political parties and the establishment of the royal dictatorship in 1938. The establishment of the dictatorship merely recorded a shift in the exercising of political power through political parties as controlled by the crown and ruling oligarchy to that of personal rule, made necessary by forcible challenge to the traditional order by the Iron Guard and its external sponsor, Nazi Germany. This challenge reflected growing dissatisfaction with the inability of political parties and the ruling class to solve the economic problems of the peasantry, the industrial workers, the urban intellectuals, and the professional students of the depression years.

The greater political mobility, employment opportunities, and economic reforms inherent in the Iron Guardist brand of populism—with its supranationalistic, anti-Semitic, and anti-minority group philosophy—threatened to alter radically the existing domestic political order and foreign political orientation. Even the fascist propagators of social and political revolution at home were, as guardians of the integrity of Greater Rumania, opposed to international collaboration with the country's irredentist neighbors. In their eyes, only bilateral relations with Nazi Germany were to be en-

[7] In addition to the works cited in note 6, consult the stimulating—if not always unbiased—studies by Lucretiu D. Patrascanu, *Sub trei dictaturi* ("Under Three Dictatorships") (Bucharest, 1945), and *Un veac de framantari sociale* ("A Century of Social Turmoil") (Bucharest, 1945). See also Hugh Seton-Watson, *Eastern Europe Between the Wars, 1918–1941* (Cambridge, 1945), pp. 198–216.

couraged. Thus the views of the challengers and of the challenged on the substance and extent of international cooperation differed only in the choice of partners.

The maintenance of territorial gains transcended all other political goals, and this supreme goal could not be realized with Rumania's own, limited, military resources. The primary area of international cooperation was thus military and political. Before the accession of Carol II in 1930 and Antonescu's dictatorship in 1940, there was little recognition of the necessity of strengthening the economic foundations of the national security system through economic and technological exchanges with other nations. The pooling of the natural resources with which Rumania is so richly endowed was generally, but not altogether, precluded by nationalist political considerations. Rumania's membership in the Little Entente, her bilateral agreements with France, Poland, and Yugoslavia, her wartime alliance with Nazi Germany and belated joining of the Allies at the end of World War II, were all forms of political and military cooperation. Instances of economic cooperation are recorded only in modest bilateral agreements with the members of the Little Entente and, of greater significance, in the blueprint for an area-wide program of economic collaboration as discussed in the Balkan conferences of the thirties. The latter scheme, although essentially subordinated to the maintenance of national integrity in the face of external political pressures, and unsuccessful on account of traditional inter-Balkan political conflicts, nevertheless provided a new concept of international cooperation. It may therefore be regarded as an antecedent to the Stoica Plan and other similar Rumanian proposals for collaboration among the Balkan nations, plans that were submitted in post-Stalinist years. A more comprehensive scheme of integration of the Rumanian economy with that of Germany was drafted and partly implemented under the Antonescu regime, in an attempt to coordinate the common war effort against the Soviet Union.

Other forms of international cooperation were even more limited in scope. In the interwar period, cultural relations were developed between Rumania and several members of the present party state system in Eastern Europe; such bilateral agreements as were concluded with Poland, Czechoslovakia, or Yugoslavia were auxiliary to political alignments. Rumania's interest in the League of Nations—most dramatically expressed in Nicolae Titulescu's pleas for broad international cooperation—was a reflection of the country's concern with national security rather than of readiness to sacrifice any of its political goals.

The extent to which Rumania shared in the decision-making process in international cooperative efforts varied with the relative strength of the partners involved. Her share of power was nominal in relations with European powers, and basically equal in the bilateral and multilateral agreements with the smaller neighboring states of Eastern Europe. Only during the military-political Balkan alliance of 1913 and the Balkan Conference meetings of the thirties did Rumania enjoy a position of power; in decisions—a result of her relative military strength in 1913 and her industrial development in the interwar period.

Compatibility of Demands Relevant to Integration

Before World War II, the Rumanian ruling élite favored integration exclusively in areas—military and

political—expressly related to the attainment and preservation of the narrow political order. Before the establishment of Greater Rumania the problem centered
on whether the Triple Alliance or the Triple Entente
offered the best alternative to territorial aggrandizement. After the establishment of Greater Rumania, the
issue of preservation again focused on the choice between the French system of alliances and the German.
The pro-French sentiments and cultural orientation,
temporarily abandoned during World War II, became
relevant again at the end of that war.

The views on integration of the rest of the politically
conscious population—the non-Rumanian bourgeoisie
and intellectuals—were incompatible with the official
doctrine. Separatism, coupled with integration into
rival or enemy states such as Hungary and Bulgaria,
was the aim of most, except for a few elements of the
Jewish communities of the Old Kingdom who sub-
scribed to pro-French internationalism. The outspoken
advocates of broad international cooperation within
the framework of the League of Nations in the twenties
and thirties were, in fact, the politicized Jewish and
Rumanian intellectuals. The Jews, motivated less by
patriotism than by the spirit of self-preservation, saw
security in the League, and in Leon Blum's France. A
nucleus of Jewish intellectuals also favored closer ties
with Russia, as they regarded communism, if not the
Soviet regime, as an equalitarian doctrine opposed to
racial or religious discrimination. Contrary to the
popular view, however, the number of Jews in the
Rumanian communist movement of the interwar years
was as infinitesimal as that of their predecessors in the
pre-1917 socialist movement. The opposition of the
politically conscious Hungarian and German elements
was far more effective in the thirties and in the early

months of World War II than the limited Jewish internationalism. The Jews were cowed into submission or destroyed; the Hungarians and Germans played a significant part in the dismemberment of Greater Rumania in 1940.

Consensus on Present and Future Integration

The relevance of the aforementioned factors for present and future international cooperation and integration is open to question. The most recent Rumanian statements on national rights and independence have been interpreted by many as a manifestation of Rumanian nationalism, a reflection of the historic opposition to the surrender of essential elements of national power.[8] But the continuing allegiance to the principle of "unity of the socialist camp" and equivocal statements on international cooperation with all nations tend to qualify (or at least modify) that contention. It is therefore appropriate to consider the present and future problems of integration and cooperation in the light of pre-communist legacy and post-World War II developments.

[8] The basic and most widely publicized statement is the so-called *Statement on the Stand of the Rumanian Workers' Party Concerning the Problems of the International Communist and Working Class Movement of April, 1964.* The complete text is contained in William E. Griffith, *Sino-Soviet Relations, 1964–1965* (Cambridge, Mass., 1967), pp. 269–96.

2. THE ENTRY OF RUMANIA INTO THE COMMUNIST PARTY-STATE SYSTEM

The fate of postwar Rumania was determined long before the conclusion of a formal peace treaty in February, 1947, and the subsequent entry of that country into the communist party-state system. From the moment the Russian armies occupied Bucharest in August, 1944, it was evident to those who were politically aware that Rumania was to be in the "Soviet sphere" after the war. The celebrated Stalin-Churchill agreement of October, 1944, which assigned "90 per cent Russian predominance" in postwar Rumania, merely confirmed the reality of the international situation.[1]

The actual seizure of power by the communists in Rumania occurred in March, 1945, when the second of two ad hoc governments, headed by military leaders, was forced to resign under Soviet pressure and was replaced by a communist-dominated regime led by Petru Groza. The possibility of any government's surviving without Russia's support was indeed remote after August, 1944. Consequently, the attempt by King Michael and the so-called traditional parties to restore constitu-

[1] The most detailed study of political developments in this period is by Ghita Ionescu, *Communism in Rumania, 1944–1962* (London, 1964), pp. 71 ff. See also Fischer-Galati, *The New Rumania*, pp. 17 ff., and Roberts, *Rumania*, pp. 242 ff.

tional government after six years of dictatorship was doomed to failure. The coup d'état staged by the king against Marshal Antonescu on August 23 was intended to preclude outright seizure of power by the advancing Russian armies. By ousting the Rumanian dictator and joining the allied powers as co-belligerents against their former ally Nazi Germany, and by establishing a coalition government dominated by the National Peasant, National Liberal, and Social Democratic parties, the king and his premier, General Constantin Sanatescu, sought to salvage a hopeless situation until all matters of war and peace could be settled at the end of the war. The acceptance by the Soviet Union of the Sanatescu coalition was formal, pending the creation of the "objective conditions," internal and external, that would allow the installation of a puppet communist regime. By November, 1944, the security provided by the agreement with Churchill and the rapid growth of the communist movement in Rumania, allowed the Russians to force a reorganization of the cabinet in a manner more favorable to communist interests. The revamped Sanatescu cabinet was brought down by Russian pressure in December, as was the government of General Radescu three months later.

Russia's relative slowness in dispensing with the Sanatescu and Radescu regimes, and for that matter, the Kremlin's toleration, until 1947, of a façade of "popular front" rule headed by a king should be ascribed to two separate factors: opposition by the United States to the Russian interpretation of the Yalta and Potsdam agreements, and the need to organize an effective communist movement in Rumania. The latter was more important than the former.

The absence of a power base for the communists can be ascribed to the outlawing of the Rumanian Communist Party in 1924 and the subsequent persecution of the illegal movement, as well as to the rejection of communist propaganda by the peasantry.[2] By August, 1944, the Rumanian Party is reputed to have had only 1,000 members. Its leadership consisted of a small nucleus of liberated political prisoners, of working-class origin, headed by Gheorghe Gheorghiu-Dej. The clandestine leaders of the communist movement of the interwar period were then in exile in the Soviet Union. Inasmuch as the Rumanian contingent was powerless and the so-called Moscow group consisted largely of non-Rumanians like Ana Pauker and Vasile Luca, and thus was clearly alien to the Rumanian people and considered discreditable by the "traditional parties" and the United States, the Kremlin chose to pursue a policy of gradual consolidation of communist power in Rumania. It encouraged those activities of the Rumanian contingent that could appeal to the population at large in the name of "social and political reform" and "democratic" order, and it supported the reliable Moscow group in its attempts to seize control of the communist movement in Rumania and carry out Stalin's directives. By March, 1945, this policy, executed under the supervision of the Russian armed forces stationed in Rumania, had persuaded the politically realistic and much of the politically unsophisticated working class and peasantry that solutions to Rumania's problems could be attained only by supporting the communists. It also assured complete control of the Rumanian Party and government by reliable servants of the Kremlin.

Although the methods of persuasion were not al-

[2] A succinct outline of the history of the communist movement in Rumania is contained in Ionescu, *Communism in Rumania,* pp. 1 ff.

ways "democratic," and the campaign against the
Sanatescu and Radescu regimes bore the imprint of
Stalin's methods, it is certain that neither Sanatescu,
Radescu, nor the traditional parties enjoyed the unequivocal support of the population. In fact, the failure of the two cabinets preceding Groza's to enact
meaningful socioeconomic legislation or to win the
allegiance of the peasantry and industrial workers
through agrarian and labor reforms facilitated the task
of the communists. Gheorghiu-Dej could carry his
message to the industrial workers; Petru Groza, the
leader of the communist-oriented Plowmen's Front, to
the peasants; and Lucretiu Patrascanu, the country's
foremost intellectual, to the educated—all with a modicum of credibility and success. The discrediting of the
interim governments and traditional parties other than
the Social Democratic, as opponents of "democracy"
and harborers of "fascism," provided the rationale for
the installation of Groza in March, 1945, and made it
difficult for the United States to object to this substitution of a "democratic" for a "fascist" order.

The Groza regime, at least through February, 1947,
continued most carefully in the process of communization for the very same reasons that prompted earlier
Soviet caution in Rumania. The communists sought
identification with the people's interests and legitimacy
as followers of the national historic tradition. In that
manner they hoped to consolidate their power in the
country and to fulfill the prerequisites, set at Yalta and
Potsdam, for recognition of and conclusion of a formal
peace treaty. Thus, the Groza regime enacted a major
agrarian reform and a series of socioeconomic measures favorable to the masses. Shortly after assuming
power, it also posed as the champion of the aspirations
of all Rumanians in securing Stalin's consent for the

reannexation of northern Transylvania in March, 1945. Evident as these maneuvers were to the initiated, they nevertheless served the purpose of persuading the population at large that communist presence in Rumania was not incompatible with the traditional desires of the population. In the same spirit, the Groza government sought to discredit the rival political parties as unrepresentative of the national interest, "fascist"-oriented, and thus expendable. The validity of these contentions and of the methods of intimidating the political opposition was "proven" in the notorious parliamentary elections of October, 1946. The communist-organized and -dominated National Democratic Front was officially reported to be the overwhelming victor over the "discredited" National Peasant and National Liberal organizations. Rigged as the election was, it nevertheless provided the Groza government with a popular mandate for the execution of its "reformist" policies, eradication of "fascism," and conclusion of a peace treaty with the victorious allies.

The political program of the Groza regime remained couched in generalities until after the signing of the treaty on February 10, 1947. Even so, it was generally understood after October, 1946, that the internal "socialist transformation" would embody the principles outlined in the Conference of the Communist Party of October, 1945, and that Rumania's foreign relations would be based on "eternal friendship" with the Soviet Union. That conference legitimized the communist movement. The Party claimed a membership of 800,000 bona fide voluntary adherents from all eligible social strata: workers, peasants, intellectuals. It also claimed legitimacy, through participation in the coup d'état of August, 1944, as the organizer of the "revolutionary liberation of Rumania from fascism," and adopted a program rooted in the history of the Rumanian communist movement and based on the historic aspirations of the Rumanian people. The Party called for the socialist industrialization of the country but made no reference to any plans for socialization of agriculture. The only "socialist" action prior to February, 1947, was the nationalization of the National Bank of Rumania, which occurred in December, 1946.

The exercise of moderation was also manifest in the degree of "satellization" required by the Soviet Union. Whereas ties with Moscow became indissoluble at both the state and party levels, total subservience came only after conclusion of the peace treaty. Before 1947, Soviet penetration and control at the state level was exercised primarily through the so-called *Sovroms*.[3] These companies—formed, allegedly, for "joint exploitation" of Rumania's natural resources and development of her petroleum, timber, uranium, and chemical industries—were established as early as 1945. That year also recorded the conclusion of the first long-term economic agreement and of the first annual trade agreement between the two countries. At the party level, Russian control manifested itself through the gradual strengthening of the number and power of the "Moscovites" in the organization and the transformation of General Secretary Gheorghiu-Dej into Stalin's most faithful servant.

All restraint ceased with the signing of the peace treaty in Paris.[4] The terms of the document itself al-

[3] The definitive study on Rumanian economic problems is by John Michael Montias, *Economic Development in Communist Rumania* (Cambridge, Mass., 1967). The reader is referred to that volume for all relevant matters in that field.

[4] The text of the treaty is contained in World Peace Foundation, *European Peace Treaties After World War II* (Boston, 1954), pp. 298–321.

lowed for the assumption of total control of the country by the Rumanian communists acting as agents of the Kremlin. Recognition by the United States and Great Britain of the legitimacy of the Groza government after the elections of October, 1946, and their readiness to sign the punitive treaty were rightly interpreted by the Soviet Union as acquiescence to the previous understanding reached by Stalin and Churchill. The customary insertion of clauses guaranteeing human rights and civil liberties were rendered meaningless by the granting to Russia of the right to collect extensive war reparations and to maintain armed forces on Rumanian territory. Similarly, the right to free political expression was nullified by the reassertion of the legitimacy of the Groza cabinet.

Whether the implementation, *à la russe,* of the provisions of the treaty was accelerated by the intensification of the cold war in the spring and summer of 1947 is a matter of continuing debate. In practical terms, the systematic reduction of Rumania to a subservient satellite of the Soviet Union started in the spring of 1947 and was completed by the time of Yugoslavia's expulsion from the "socialist camp" one year later. During that period Stalin ordered Rumania's rejection of the Marshall Plan and a cutting of all ties with the West (June, 1947); the abolition of the monarchy and establishment of a "People's Democratic Republic" (December, 1947); the conclusion of a treaty of political, economic, and cultural vassalage—the so-called Treaty of Friendship, Cooperation, and Mutual Assistance between the U.S.S.R. and the Rumanian People's Republic—for a period of twenty years (February, 1948); condemnation of Tito's heresy (June, 1948), and, in general, unequivocal subservience to the Kremlin.

Internally, the Rumanian communists, acting on behalf of Stalin's or their own interests, destroyed all political opposition. First, they outlawed the National Peasant and National Liberal parties and convicted their leaders, in 1947, of "anti-state" activities. Then, after the establishment of the republic, they incorporated the Social Democratic organization into the unitary Rumanian Workers' (Communist) Party in March, 1948. The nationalization of industry, banking, insurance, mining, and transportation enterprises was ordered in June, 1948, and state planning was begun in July of that year. With these actions Rumania made its entry into the socialist-state system as a faithful member of the Soviet empire. Certain basic changes in the country's physical, demographic, social, and belief structures, which had occurred since August, 1944, assumed a seemingly irrevocable character. In any case, these changes clearly affected the integration potential and goals of the Rumanian communist state.

Ecological-physical Factors and Demographic Structure

Ratification of the loss of Bessarabia and northern Bukovina to the Soviet Union by the Paris Peace Treaty, in February, 1947, facilitated the satellization of Rumania. The redrawing of the Western borders of the U.S.S.R. with Rumania, and other members of the Soviet bloc, nullified Rumania's power of resistance to absorption by the bloc as she was surrounded on all but the southwestern side by member states. The basic demographic structure was not substantially altered until the country's "socialist transformation" began in earnest in the summer of 1948. The immediate post-war changes resulted from the loss, through resettlement or emigration, of much of the German and Jewish population. Regardless of religious affiliation, the demographic factors became irrelevant to any consideration of popular influence on the regime's policies of integration into the Stalinist bloc.

Belief System and Social System

Between August, 1944, and July, 1948, the traditional belief and social systems were radically altered to facilitate close cooperation with the Soviet Union and the People's Democracies of Eastern Europe. The new goals, anticipated as early as 1945 and proclaimed formally in the Soviet-type constitution of April, 1948, made the construction of socialism and the socialist transformation of society in accordance with the Soviet example the *raison d'être* of Rumania and its peoples.[5] Emulation of the Soviet Union entailed rejection of all nationalist and bourgeois values and goals of the past. The cultural orientation of Rumania's inhabitants, regardless of ethnic origin, was redirected toward the Soviet Union. Western ties, whether Latinist, French, or other, were suspect and inadmissible. The attack on religion, which started in 1947, was direct and forceful; religion had to become an instrument of state policy. Nationalism, in its "bourgeois-chauvinist" aspects, was unequivocally condemned and rejected. Rumania's previous self-image—that of a bastion of Latin civilization in the Balkans—was de-

[5] The text of the Constitution of April 13, 1948, is contained in Jan F. Triska, ed., *Constitutions of the Communist Party-States* (Stanford, 1968), pp. 350–61. Interpretations of its significance in developments of that period may be found in Ionescu, *Communism in Rumania,* pp. 71 ff., and Fischer-Galati, *The New Rumania,* pp. 17 ff.

stroyed. By 1948 the Rumanian People's Republic was officially a member of the family of revolutionary, communist nations headed by the "glorious Soviet Union." Only association with other members of this august community was permitted—in short, with nations comprising the Soviet bloc. In case of any crisis, national or international, the Soviet armies would offer the necessary protection to the Rumanian communist regime.

The transformation of the social system, which assumed a revolutionary character after July, 1948, had proceeded slowly before that time. The peasants were allowed to retain private ownership of their land, and no pressure was put on the villages to provide manpower for industry. In 1947, however, the poor peasant class in the villages organized for the purpose of destroying the "kulaks" and the other components of the rural élite, teachers and priests. The first major action against the "wealthy peasants" was the currency reform of August, 1947, characterized by unequal reevaluation of the currency according to the relative wealth of the population. Nevertheless, that reform did not break the "kulaks" any more than it destroyed the economic bases of the other social class marked for extinction, the commercial and industrial bourgeoisie. Until the nationalization of industry, the bourgeoisie was subject only to financial and cultural harassment. But the spectre of economic disaster, political extinction, and class warfare was clear to the middle class after the adoption of the Constitution of 1948 and the promised "socialist transformation" of the country. The same fate was feared by the nontechnological professional groups—particularly teachers, lawyers, writers, and creative artists—and members of the private and public bureaucracy. The growing demands for intellectual and social conformity and attacks on "elements hostile to the working people" singled out professional people of "unhealthy" social origin and political orientation. As the vast majority of the professional cadres were vulnerable on both counts, they were nervously awaiting the social revolution that seemed inevitable in the summer of 1948. Only the "technocrats" appeared secure, because their special skills would be required for the impending industrialization of Rumania. They were to be the beneficiaries of the forthcoming "socialist transformation"—together with the industrial working class, which, in mid-1948, was still numerically small, unskilled, and underpaid.

Economic System

The alternation of the economic system had only begun by the summer of 1948, but the blueprint for nationalization was clear. The nationalization law of June 11, 1948, called for acquisition, theoretically with compensation to the owners, of all enterprises of "national economic importance" in the petroleum, textile, timber, and metallurgical industries, as well as of the majority of all banks, trade, and insurance companies.[6] The law was implemented shortly after issuance.

Similarly, the establishment of a State Planning Commission on July 18, 1948, did not mean the immediate centralization of all economic activity; but the radical transformation of the economic order was imminent. It was also clear by 1948 that the transformation of the economy was to be carried out only within

[6] A convenient summary of these measures and of their significance may be found in Ionescu, *Communism in Rumania,* pp. 161 ff.

the Soviet bloc and with resources available within that bloc. The Rumanian economy was irrevocably tied to the Russian by virtue of the economic provisions of the peace treaty and by short- and long-range economic agreements. It was also firmly tied to the economies of other members of the Soviet empire through short- and long-term trade and economic cooperation conventions—with Bulgaria, Czechoslovakia, Poland, and Hungary—concluded in 1947 and 1948. The only possible avenue to independence was through similar agreements with Yugoslavia; but that road was closed after Tito's defection from the bloc in July, 1948.

Rumania as a Self-fulfilling Unit

The goals set by 1948 by the only group that mattered—the communist élite—could not be attained independently with Rumania's own resources, given the externally imposed orders and limitations. The exploitation of the country's natural resources for the attainment of Rumanian goals was not permitted by Moscow since these resources were earmarked for the reconstruction of the Soviet Union. In short, the exploitation of socialism rather than its construction in Rumania was the cardinal aim of Moscow and her Rumanian agents.

Under these circumstances the areas and types of integration and international cooperation were externally dictated, giving Rumania virtually no share in the decision-making process. As rulers of a satellite within the Soviet international empire, the Russian-imposed agents in Rumania merely carried out orders. In many instances, however, the new communist élite genuinely endorsed the need for Rumanian integration with other communist party states. Close economic, political, and cultural ties between the U.S.S.R. and her satellites were sought for protection against "imperialists" and for the attainment of the common socialist goals, yet no specific forms of multilateral integration were devised or permitted by the Soviet Union. Bilateralism, primarily in the form of unilateral Soviet exploitation of the satellites, was the limit of integration condoned by Moscow.[7]

Compatibility of Demands Relevant to Integration

The basic question raised in connection with integration into *"Satellitenstaat"* is that of the conflict between traditional and new Rumanian political élites during the years immediately preceding the country's entry into the communist party-state system. The grave nature of this conflict is evidenced by the endless political trials and the imprisonment without trial of leading members of the "traditional" political organizations. Former leaders, as well as many followers and associates, were accused of plotting against the new order and summarily removed from the political and public scene. It is a valid assumption that, at least before the peace treaty, the majority of the politically conscious population, with the exception of the Communist Party and a few minor allied groupings such as the Plowmen's Front and splinter groups of the Social Democratic Party, was adamantly opposed to forced integration with the Soviet Union and other members of the bloc. However, this opposition was primarily motivated by traditional antagonisms and hatred of

[7] Of particular value on these points is the chapter on "Rumania and the Economic Integration of Eastern Europe" contained in Montias, *Economic Development,* pp. 187 ff.

the Rumanian communist regime and its Russian sponsors, rather than by any rational analysis of the possible advantages that might be derived from closer cooperation with Russia and the people's democracies. Indeed, no such advantages were apparent at the time of Rumania's formal entry into the communist party-state system in 1948, given the ruthless economic exploitation of the country by Russia, in addition to her adamant insistence on repayment of the war damages exacted by the Treaty of Paris.[8] The principle of integration with other nations was accepted in varying degrees by certain segments of the population, such as the technological and bureaucratic cadres of the new order, and the ruling élite. This acceptance is indeed the key to any analysis of the integration potential and inclinations of Rumania at that time and in later years.

Little has been written about the impact of the Marshall Plan on Rumania, other than a contemporary recording of the Rumanian regime's of crude rejection of its terms. But subsequently released materials reveal that a substantial segment of the ruling élite favored the principle of broader international cooperation with the technologically advanced nations, if such cooperation would speed the socialist transformation of their country. Indeed, at the time of the 1952 purging of Ana Pauker, Vasile Luca, and Teohari Georgescu, Moscow's principal agents in Rumania, the core of the present-day leadership accused Pauker and her cohorts of sabotaging the goals set by the Party in 1945. These goals, involving the socialist transformation of the country in all respects, with primary emphasis on industrialization, were to be realized not only through

[8] Ionescu provides an extensive cost-analysis of Rumania's indebtedness to the Soviet Union, indicating that in 1946, for example, it amounted to $1,050,000,000. Ionescu, *Communism in Rumania,* pp. 136–39.

exclusive cooperation with the U.S.S.R. and other communist states but with all who were ready to co-operate without challenging the communist order and its aims. Thus, according to Gheorghiu-Dej's state-ments of 1952, the principle of international coopera-tion for economic advancement had been proclaimed in 1945.[9] This principle had been endorsed in the same year by other political groups, primarily the So-cial Democrats, who indeed envisaged the economic development of Rumania through closer ties with all Allied nations. The ravages of the war and the realities of the international situation in 1945 tended, in the eyes of realists, to minimize the necessity for interna-tionalism of the prewar variety, and to maximize the need for nonpolitical ties in order to prevent Ru-mania's complete domination by the U.S.S.R. and its agents. Russian imperialism, having precluded any con-nections with the non-Russian bloc, silenced the aspira-tions of the noncommunists as well as Rumanian or Western-oriented Party members, and forced rejection of the Marshall Plan in 1947. The question remains not only whether these groups were successfully si-lenced but whether the Rumanian communist leader-ship itself was altogether in favor of exclusive coopera-tion with the Soviet bloc in 1947–48.

[9] A detailed account of the contemporary accusations is con-tained in the June 6, 1953, issue of *For a Lasting Peace, For a People's Democracy*. An interesting contemporary analysis en-titled "The Stratagem of Abuse" will be found in *News From Behind the Iron Curtain*, I, no. 6 (June, 1952), 1–4. Gheorghiu-Dej's subsequent recapitulation of the events of 1952 and their antecedents is contained in his "Report to the Central Commit-tee of the Rumanian Workers' Party, November 30–December 5, 1961," whose original text in Rumanian may be found in *Scinteia* of December 7, 1961. A recent re-evaluation of the significance of these problems is found in Fischer-Galati, *The New Rumania*, pp. 38–43.

It is evident that no element of choice existed: consequently no alternatives were sought by the ruling élite. For security reasons the regime could not allow any contacts with the member nations of the Marshall Plan, particularly since opponents of communism looked upon that plan as a gateway to "liberation." In the name of national security, the Rumanian leaders actively and sincerely promoted the establishment of closer political and cultural ties with the U.S.S.R. and other members of the bloc. At first it was imperative to extirpate all traces of chauvinism and "bourgeois nationalism" in Rumania that might threaten the regime's existence; but these precautions became less necessary as Moscow succeeded in exerting greater control within the Soviet bloc. By 1948 all countries bordering on Rumania were in the Soviet sphere, and it made little difference to a disgruntled member of a "coinhabiting nationality" whether he was living in Hungary, Bulgaria, Poland, Russia, or Rumania; national affiliation ceased to be an escapist feature. However, affirmation of ties with previous or new "friends," such as France, the United States, and the West in general, did pose a potential threat to the regime. The Rumanian rulers therefore rejected all connections with the West, notwithstanding their awareness of the advantages inherent in limited economic relations with the "imperialist camp." Flexibility in international relations presupposed not only internal stability but also a modicum of independence from the U.S.S.R.

3: INTENSIVE SOCIALIST DEVELOPMENT OF RUMANIA: STALINISM

The socialist transformation of Rumania, according to Stalin's precepts and the basic Rumanian blueprint, the Constitution of April, 1948, was all but completed by the time of Stalin's death. The transformation was radical and affected all aspects of Rumanian life. But by 1953 the bases for a Rumanian "road to socialism," albeit Stalinist, had been firmly established. Superficially, the red thread in the transformation of the country was the indiscriminate adoption of Soviet models, whether appropriate or not. In reality, the crucial aspects of the process of communization were the retention of power by the Rumanian communists and the forging, by them, of a Rumanian communist state which differed in at least one essential respect from the Russian.

The radical transformation of the country was most apparent in the socioeconomic area.[1] The nationalization of industry and the planning of the economy, which started with two one-year plans in 1949 and 1950 and the first Five-Year Plan for 1951–55, accelerated modernization. Most of the capital investments

[1] A convenient survey of these developments is contained in Ionescu, *Communism in Rumania*, pp. 165 ff.

went into heavy industry (36.8 per cent) and the transportation system (21.2 per cent), at the expense of consumer goods, agriculture, and housing. Though these allocations aggravated the plight of the population in general, they provided the means for extremely rapid industrial growth. By 1950 total Rumanian industrial production had reached the 1938 level (in January, 1948, the level had been only 75 per cent of 1938). By 1953 Rumania's industrial production was 2.7 times greater than in 1938. The production of consumer goods proceeded at a much slower rate, but still was nearly twice as large in 1953 as in 1938.[2] These statistics, however, hide the fact that the rising social and economic requirements of the population were not met in a satisfactory manner. With industrialization, the urban population grew from 3,713,139 in 1948 to 4,424,000 in 1953 and put tremendous pressure on housing facilities and food supplies. Housing was worse than inadequate: only 872 apartments were built in Bucharest between 1949 and 1952 for an influx of population in excess of 250,000. Food supplies were also deficient, primarily because of the peasants' opposition to a low price structure for their produce and, after 1949, to the beginning of agricultural collectivization. And in all instances, the salaries of the newly created industrial labor force were too low to permit satisfaction of even rudimentary socioeconomic needs. These factors increased the hostility of the population toward the Rumanian communist leadership and the Soviet Union, the primary beneficiary of Rumania's economic growth. Indeed, such foreign trade as existed was primarily with the U.S.S.R. itself (70 per cent of

[2] Interesting details and a careful analysis of industrial development in that period are contained in Montias, *Economic Development,* pp. 23 ff.

total foreign trade), at prices and conditions distinctly detrimental to Rumania. The rest of the trade, at relatively better prices, was entirely with members of the Soviet bloc.[3]

The dissatisfaction of the industrial working class mattered little to the communist regime; they were still small in number (in the vicinity of 1,000,000 in 1953 as compared to 750,000 in 1938) and could be rewarded by membership in the Rumanian Workers' Party and by other ideological and material benefits. But the displeasure of the peasantry over the betrayal of the principles of the reform of 1945 and the oft-repeated assurances that collectivization was not contemplated, posed graver problems to the communists. In practical terms, the collectivization of agriculture decreed in March, 1949, was designed to created the basis for effective agricultural production commensurate with the industrial development of the country and to carry the social revolution to the "bourgeois-oriented" village. Collectivization enjoyed a modicum of success in its first objective, despite opposition by the peasantry. The process of socialization of the land was slow and tedious, but by 1953 collective farms and agricultural associations of the TOZ type were more productive than the still predominant private sector. Moreover, the gradual mechanization of agriculture and development of model state farms had by 1953 raised the level of production to that of prewar Rumania. That objective was attained only by force, because of the tremendous resistance of the peasantry to socialization. The physical annihilation of "kulaks," the *de facto* confiscation of agricultural produce in the name of compulsory

[3] Agricultural problems and foreign trade questions are discussed and analyzed by Montias, *Economic Development,* pp. 87 ff.

deliveries and through arbitrary price structures, and the general attack on traditional values identified with religion and the family, brought the villages to the verge of revolution by 1953. By that time, the peasant had not been subdued, and agricultural problems were still plaguing the regime, but the kulaks had been eliminated.

By 1953 the fate of the bourgeoisie and professional class had been settled. Private commerce had been eliminated and the commercial bourgeoisie financially ruined. All professional groups, except physicians, had been reduced to the status of state employees. Those of "suspect social origin" were barred from any employment commensurate with their training and were generally forced to engage in manual labor or other menial jobs. The threat of, or actuality of, imprisonment for any conceivable offense against the "socialist order" were all-pervasive phenomena. A new society was being created by eradication of the "class enemy" and introduction of new "socialist values." These values were inculcated by a revamped educational system and a new, socialist, culture.

The educational system was recast to insure the training of the cadres required for socialist construction and their indoctrination in communist values and ideology.[4] Technical schools, trade schools, and schools for unskilled workers were set up throughout Rumania at the expense of the traditional theoretical elementary and secondary schools. New universities and institutions of higher learning were also created. The efficiency of the educational system was below expectations, for the masses admitted to the various

[4] On the transformation of the educational system see Stephen Fischer-Galati, "Education," ed. Stephen Fischer-Galati, *Romania,* pp. 148–64.

schools were largely illiterate, as were the makeshift teachers who replaced the suspect members of the academic profession. The mass purging of teachers, and the restrictions imposed on the admission of children of nonproletarian or peasant origin, proved detrimental to the training of competent cadres, but facilitated the process of indoctrination. By 1953, however, the manpower requirements were generally met, and destruction of the "bourgeois" values and influences that had traditionally emanated from Rumanian schools was complete.[5]

Rumanian intellectuals and artists who had not been associated or identified with "fascism" became the disseminators of "socialist realism" for the masses. The others were purged and their earlier writings or artistic creations banned. Even Rumanian classical writers fell into disgrace because of their "bourgeois-nationalist" prejudices and, on occasion, anti-Russian and pro-Western attitudes. Religion, historically identified with nationalism and anticommunism, was drafted into the service of the state.[6] When the required conformity to socialist realism was rejected by religious leaders, or when the leaders and parish priests themselves were suspect, more radical measures were used. Thus, the Concordat of 1927, which regulated relations between the Roman Catholic Church and the Rumanian government, was unilaterally abrogated in July, 1948, and Catholic cultural and educational activities were terminated. The Rumanian Uniate (Greek Catholic Church), which had approximately 1,500,000 members and had functioned in Transylvania since the late seventeenth century, was dissolved by decree in December, 1948, and incorporated into the Rumanian Orthodox

[5] Consult Fischer-Galati, *Romania,* pp. 165–81.
[6] *Ibid.,* pp. 132 ff.

Church. The lesser denominations fared better but, invariably, church attendance was discouraged, and all churches became instruments for dissemination of communist propaganda, occasionally in biblical terms.

The socioeconomic and related cultural revolution were completed by 1953, as was the all important political revolution. The formal, constitutional, and institutional changes emulated Soviet prototypes. The Constitution of 1948 was closely patterned on the Stalinist Constitution of 1936 and was almost identical with similar fundamental laws in Albania, Bulgaria, or Hungary. The entrenchment of the one-party state; the establishment of a mock parliament, the Grand National Assembly, and of a powerless presidium, the collective presidency of the Republic; the reorganization of the organs of local government through the establishment of people's councils—all were significant in providing the Party with total control of the country's political life and government.[7] Even the Council of Ministers, which structurally resembled the pre-entry council, was staffed by members of the Party's highest organs and acted merely as an executor of the decisions of the Party. Similarly, the revamped system of state security and the small military establishment (limited to approximately 150,000 men by the Peace Treaty of Paris) were modern versions of prewar equivalents whose function was to maintain the authority of the communist regime in Rumania and extirpate all actual or potential opposition. By 1953, the Party was the all-powerful and sole political organization; even tacit opposition had ended. And at least superficially, the Rumanian Party and government seemed committed

[7] A good summary of these changes is contained in Ionescu, *Communism in Rumania,* pp. 156 ff. See also Triska, *Constitutions,* pp. 362 ff.

to the role of satellite to the Russian Party and government. The Kremlin's directives were followed blindly at home by trusted leaders like Gheorghiu-Dej, the Party's General Secretary, Ana Pauker and Vasile Luca, the leaders of the Moscovite contingent, all other members of the Politburo and Central Committee, and lesser officials. The rank and file of the Party, which comprised some 1,000,000 members, had no voice in determining policies and merely carried out orders from above. In foreign affairs there was no deviation from Moscow's policies. The annual cultural and trade agreements between Rumania and the members of the Soviet bloc were renewed as a matter of course; condemnation of "imperialists," Titoists, and all other enemies of the socialist camp was more virulent in Rumania than in Moscow.[8] The loss of national and political identity seemed complete by 1953. But this was a deceptive impression since under the surface of conformity and subservience a major and decisive struggle for power was taking place within the Rumanian Workers' Party between the "Rumanians" and the "Moscovites." This struggle within political organization was to decide the country's future after Stalin's death.[9]

It is now known that, from as early as 1947–48, the so-called Rumanian group, headed by Gheorghiu-Dej and made up of his former associates of the pre-1945 period, was much less pro-Russian in its orientation than the Moscow group, headed by Ana Pauker and her Moscow-trained supporters. It is also known that the struggle developing between these groups centered

[8] A list of the principal treaties concluded between Rumania and members of the Soviet bloc in this period may be found in Fischer-Galati, *Romania*, pp. 382 ff.

[9] A careful analysis of these factors is contained in Fischer-Galati, *The New Rumania*, pp. 35 ff.

on the question of Rumania's position and role in the Soviet empire, and consequently, on the extent of the Party's authority to determine national and international policies and to implement the goals first formulated in 1945.

Belief System and Social System

This issue came into the open only in 1952, during the Korean War, when the Rumanian group emerged victorious and proclaimed that the national goal of the Rumanian Workers' Party and of the Rumanian people was the attainment of socialism on the basis of the 1945 blueprint. Certain "objective factors" favoring broader international cooperation with party states, as well as with nonmember nations of the socialist camp, were cited by the victorious group as relevant to their action and decision. These factors were directly connected with alterations in the country's traditional belief system that occurred during the Stalinist period, reflecting the forcible social-demographic transformations imposed by the regime. The industrialization of society revolutionized the countryside and markedly decreased the ratio of urban to rural population. By 1952 more than 10 per cent of the rural population had moved into towns, joining the ranks of the industrial proletariat. Through mass indoctrination, the urban workers became conscious of the international nature of the industrialization process and of the need not only for cooperation with other communist nations for the attainment of the socialist society but for overcoming nationalist prejudices and nonsocialist ways of thought as well.

The same propaganda was conducted, with markedly less success, in the villages. These new views rejecting religion, nationalism, and ethnic prejudices transcended national considerations of the older type. An international outlook, loosely defined as "proletarian internationalism," was the aim. The effectiveness of these condemnations of past values and affiliations must have been limited, considering most recent developments, but it is safe to assume that the relentless indoctrination and the realities of industrialization did transform the traditional belief system to a large extent.

The basic goal of the regime—the socialist transformation of society—was apparently shared by the entire ruling élite, who differed only over the means of attaining it. The goal was unacceptable to the peasantry, however; they adamantly opposed the "socialist transformation of agriculture" despite educational efforts and police repression. The technical cadres and industrial working class, in spite of the frustrations and hardships of dictated industrialization, supported the goal.

Degree of Integration of Rumania with Other Systems

As industrialization progressed, the principle of international cooperation in the economic and technological fields became widely accepted. Industrial progress also brought the growing realization that Rumania's economic exploitation by the Soviet Union was most detrimental to the attainment of the aims of the government. This fact was best understood by the technological and bureaucratic cadres and by the intelligentsia, who favored reduction of economic subservience to Russia on the expectation that such action could bring about some relaxation of internal pressures exerted by Gheorghiu-Dej's Stalinist regime. In their opinion, ties with countries outside the Soviet bloc, including contacts with Tito's Yugoslavia as well as other party and nonparty states, would enhance the possibilities of liberalization at home. It is for this reason that the Rumanian group gained a modicum of popular support in 1952; directing its offensive against the obvious stooges of the Soviet Union, this group urged the attainment of national goals by the peoples of Rumania, with the assistance of Moscow as opposed to exclusive dependence upon the Soviet leaders. The assertion of the "national" nature of the communist goal, to be attained through a Rumanian effort in close cooperation with the international communist movement and the party states, gave the country a well-defined status and eliminated the much-discussed possibility of Rumania's transformation into a Soviet republic.[10]

It would be erroneous, however, to assume that in 1952 Gheorghiu-Dej and his close associates seriously entertained the possibility of pursuing international policies at variance with Soviet dictates. Rumania remained a Russian satellite, and its freedom of cooperation was restricted to the Soviet-controlled party states of Eastern Europe; international connections had to be *en famille*. Nevertheless, there were elements of contradiction in the regime's aim of attaining socialism at home and its inability to reduce dependence on the Soviet Union, since Russia was in effect the principal

[10] A comprehensive review of these problems may be found in Stephen Fischer-Galati, "Rumania: A Dissenting Voice in the Balkans," in *Issues of World Communism,* ed. Andrew Gyorgy (Princeton, 1966), pp. 128–31.

impediment to the attainment of the goals of 1945 as restated in 1952. Technological and economic ties with the West were essential to the attainment of the "national" goals, a fact that was clearly realized by Gheorghiu-Dej. The question remained whether international cooperation might be achieved without renewing at least some of the traditional ties. In short, could Gheorghiu-Dej's Rumania, if dedicated to international cooperation for the attainment of her goals, extend this internationalism to nonparty states without jeopardizing the internal security of the regime and incurring the wrath of the U.S.S.R.? Although the basic problems are still to be resolved, tentative solutions became possible after Stalin's death.

4: THE THAW

The first significant manifestation was the adoption of the "New Course" in August, 1953, an overt admission that the extreme pressure placed on the national resources and economic machine by Stalinist requests had to be relaxed, and a more rational economic policy adopted.[1] Indicative of the scope of this change was the dissolution of the *Sovroms* and the new emphasis placed on the production of consumer goods, designed to satisfy the minimal domestic requirements. However, official policies continued to stress rapid socialization of agriculture; and Russian-imposed and -oriented patterns dominated cultural intellectual activities, suppressing national manifestations regarded in any way as bourgeois. In short, there was to be no liberalization in any area that might jeopardize the stability of the regime. The policies of

[1] A penetrating review of post-1952 conditions and problems is contained in Gheorghiu-Dej's report to the Second Congress of the Rumanian Workers' Party on December 23, 1955, which is contained in Gheorghe Gheorghiu-Dej, *Articole si cuvintari (decembrie 1955–iulie 1959)* ("Articles and Speeches, December 1955–July 1959") (Bucharest, 1959), pp. 6 ff. An informative and intelligent analysis of the "New Course" may be found in *News From Behind the Iron Curtain,* III, no. 7 (July, 1954), 3–11.

the New Course reflected solely a reappraisal of Rumania's economic potential to attain the "national" goal. This re-evaluation, completed in 1955, resulted in two separate formulas for cooperation and integration with other states, and the tentative formulation of a third principle, that of "peaceful coexistence" *à la roumaine,* now the distinctive feature of Rumanian international relations. These decisions of 1955 were realistically conceived in terms of the domestic and foreign factors affecting international cooperation and integration.

In the simplest terms, as expressed that year by Gheorghiu-Dej at the Second Party Congress, the Rumanian regime favored international cooperation with all nations, regardless of their social systems, provided that the principles of international equality and of noninterference in domestic affairs were recognized.[2] These relations, defined as "of the new type," were to be developed primarily among members of the socialist camp, but "coexistence" with nonparty states was also desired. The areas of international cooperation would be determined by the nations concerned, although as far as the Rumanian regime was concerned, the preferred spheres were military and economic. The limits of cooperation indicated by Gheorghiu-Dej reflected the motivations of the Rumanian communist leadership in seeking diversification and redefinition of its international relations. The so-called Rumanian independent course, which became evident only in the early sixties, was actually initiated after Khrushchev's ascendancy in the U.S.S.R. and the first ascertainable manifestations of Sino-Soviet friction. The motivations of Gheorghiu-Dej and his close associates were basically

[2] Gheorghiu-Dej, *Articole si cuvintari,* pp. 69 ff.

political.[3] Identified as they were with Stalinism, their power could be threatened by a more liberal leadership in Moscow and by decrease in the number of Stalinist members in the Rumanian Workers' Party. The threat of Khrushchevism was evident to Gheorghiu-Dej from as early as 1954, and the initial measures of political self-preservation date from that year. The doctrine of "relations of the new type" was tentatively adopted in 1954, and the basic identification of Rumanian interests with the Chinese—both measures opposed to Khrushchevism—was first stated in the exchange of telegrams on the occasion of the tenth anniversary of Rumania's liberation (on August 23) stressing national self-determination within the socialist camp.

The need to seek identification with the national historic tradition and to attain historic legitimacy as a *Rumanian* state, albeit socialist, was an essential requirement for assertion of the doctrine of "relations of the new type" within the socialist community of nations. It is doubtful that the reopening of Rumania's borders to noncommunists from the West, and related statements on coexistence were—or for that matter could have been—intended to seek alternative roads to socialism or political and economic bridges to nations inimical to the U.S.S.R. But it should be assumed that the equating of the Party's interests and policies with those of the Rumanian state was designed to secure the allegiance of the people to the "Rumanian" leadership of Gheorghiu-Dej as against "internationalist, cosmopolitan," probably pro-Khrushchev elements in the Rumanian Party. Thus, the major tenets, na-

[3] A detailed analysis of these problems is contained in Fischer-Galati, *The New Rumania,* pp. 44 ff.

tional and international, of communist nationalism—
or Gheorghiu-Dejism—were formulated by 1955. They
affected Rumania's policies toward integration with
other systems for years to come.

Degree of Integration of Rumania with Other Systems

The maintenance of internal stability and of the
international communist party-state system in Eastern
Europe remained a question of fundamental concern
to the Rumanian regime. But it also created dilemmas
and contradictions. Thus, the conclusion of the Warsaw Pact in 1955 was enthusiastically supported, even
though the military agreement entailed subordination
of the Rumanian to the Soviet military machine.[4] The
military integration of the bloc recognized the principle of equality among the members of the alliance to
an infinitely greater degree than had the bilateral alliances of the Stalinist period. Russia's regarding military integration as a corollary to economic integration
under COMECON posed more serious problems for
the Rumanian leadership. The reactivation of COME-
CON, which had operated as a shallow and meaningless façade for direct Russian exploitation of the East
European satellites since its establishment in 1949, did
in fact test Rumania's proclivities toward integration
in the Soviet bloc.[5]

The extent to which the Rumanian regime endorsed

[4] An excellent review of matters related to military integration will be found in Robin A. Remington, *The Changing
Soviet Perception of the Warsaw Pact* (Cambridge, Mass., 1967),
pp. 7 ff.

[5] On COMECON consult Montias, *Economic Development,*
pp. 187 ff.

COMECON in 1954 is not clear. Gheorghiu-Dej and his associates apparently regarded the *primus inter pares* relationship as preferable to previous Stalinist ties, given the lack of viable alternate solutions to Rumania's economic problems, and her enormous dependence on Soviet economic and military support. Insofar as economic integration was loose in form and long range in purpose, the initially favorable Rumanian response to the reactivation of COMECON does not offer an accurate barometer of the regime's intentions. In any case, the Rumanians did not regard participation in COMECON as prohibiting the development of "relations of the new type" with non-member nations. In fact, the regime had concluded its first significant economic agreements with the industrial West in 1954, and established the first meaningful economic contacts with party states in the Far East, including China and North Korea. It is noteworthy that the value of Rumania's trade with noncommunist countries had reached nearly $60,000,000 by 1955 (in contrast to $35,400,000 in 1951), approximately 20 per cent of the country's total foreign trade. The Rumanians seemed anxious to broaden the scope of their international economic relations, preferably on a bilateral basis, although the principle of economic integration in COMECON was not rejected or even challenged at that time.

International cooperation outside the socialist camp in activities other than economic was not sought. The common cultural milieu of the Soviet bloc, based on "socialist realism," could not be altered without jeopardizing the security of the Party and state. The "correctness" of the regime's views was proven in 1956 at the time of the Hungarian revolution. The basic opposition of the inhabitants of Rumania to Moscow and the domestic communist regime was expressed in pro-Hungarian manifestations in Transylvania, much of whose Magyar population demanded reincorporation of that province into a Free Hungary, and in student demonstrations in Bucharest and Iasi, aimed at the restoration of the traditional French and Western cultural ties and the abandonment of the exclusively pro-Russian ideological and cultural orientation. But these "bourgeois-nationalist" manifestations were skillfully rechanneled into "socialist patriotism" by a Rumanian regime bent on exploiting the crisis of 1956 to its own advantage.[6]

The regime, aware not only of the survival of "bourgeois-nationalist" tendencies in Transylvania and elsewhere but also of the improbability of repetition of "1956" in Eastern Europe, adopted its own carrot-and-stick policy. Bourgeois-nationalism and Western provocation in Hungary and elsewhere in Eastern Europe were fiercely denounced, and cultural liberalization in the form of renewed ties with the reactionary West unequivocally rejected. However, while strictly prohibiting any deviation from socialist realism, the Party allowed the introduction of "patriotic" themes into literary and artistic productions. Moreover, intellectuals who had been barred from professional activities because of "unhealthy" social origin or ideological commitments were gradually reinstated on condition of strict adherence to the Party line.

To consolidate his own position vis-à-vis Moscow—which was forced during the Hungarian crisis to ac-

---

[6] On "1956" in Rumania and the regime's reaction to the Hungarian revolution consult Gheorghiu-Dej, *Articole si cuvintari,* pp. 248–68. See also Fischer-Galati, *The New Rumania,* pp. 62 ff.

knowledge the theoretical equality of all members of the socialist camp—and to build a basis for stronger popular support at home, Gheorghiu-Dej also proclaimed the need for radical economic improvements, including a rising standard of living for the masses, goals which were to be attained by economic cooperation with all nations on the basis of "relations of the new type" and "mutual advantages." In this respect he could be persuasive, considering the significant improvement in the country's economy recorded by the end of 1956. The Plenum of the Central Committee met in December of that year and reviewed the achievements which indicated a tremendous rise in industrial production since 1953. In heavy industry, for example, the production of power, fuel, and building materials more than doubled; and even in the consumer goods sector, increases of 150 per cent were not uncommon. Nevertheless, considering the continuing growth of the urban population (from 3,713,-139 in 1948 to 5,474,264 in 1956) and the general growth rate from 15,872,624 inhabitants in 1948 to 17,489,450 in 1956, the supplies of consumer goods and foodstuffs and the general wage scale remained inadequate. These discrepancies were remedied by the Plenum by reducing capital investment in heavy industry while increasing it in consumer goods, raising wages, and abolishing the system of compulsory deliveries in agriculture.[7] The collectivization drive was intensified; but persuasion and financial and technical aid replaced brute force in this "socialist" search for ways to improve the efficiency of agriculture and increase the general well-being of the population. These measures and principles, in effect, weakened the possi-

[7] On these measures and their significance consult Ionescu, *Communism in Rumania,* pp. 275 ff.

bility of close economic integration through COME-CON, inasmuch as that organization could not provide the most effective means for attaining the economic and political goals of the regime. Rumania then sought to gain safety for its infantile autarchic tendencies by championing the unity of the socialist camp in general, as opposed to mere unity of the Soviet bloc, while advocating the extension of peaceful coexistence with all nations in Western Europe, the Middle East, Africa, and elsewhere, who were willing to engage in "relations of the new type." The principle of broad international relations in the economic field was firmly restated in 1957 in Rumania's interpretation of the principles of the Moscow Declaration of that year.[8] By this time, the regime's views on such matters were generally acceptable to the majority of the population.

Compatibility of Demands Relevant to Integration

The Hungarian revolution made most Rumanians realize that any changes in the domestic as well as in the international position of the country would have to be entrusted to the leadership of the Rumanian Workers' Party. Whatever hopes of "liberation" or "liberalization" the anticommunist population might have entertained were frustrated by the events of 1956. In effect, those who had been politically active prior to the establishment of the communist state, as well as those nurturing hopes for the restoration of a political order different from the prevalent power struc-

[8] Gheorghiu-Dej, *Articole si cuvintari,* pp. 336–49.

ture, lost all expectation of "liberation"; coexistence with Gheorghiu-Dej's regime became a necessary reality. Those intellectuals, professional people, bureaucrats, and technical cadres who had made their peace with the regime, hoping for liberalization through the restoration of cultural, if not political, ties with the West, knew in 1956 that this could not be attained. The most that could be hoped for after the Hungarian revolution was a lessening of dependence upon the Soviet Union, a broader network of international relations in nonsensitive areas, and in a negative context, the possible development of difficulties within the socialist camp that might be exploited by the Rumanian leadership to its advantage. In other words, the "relations of the new type" and "coexistence" formulas, as first stated by Gheorghiu-Dej in 1953 and reconfirmed both in 1956 and in the interpretation of the Moscow Declaration of 1957, were *faute de mieux* acceptable to the Rumanians. The statements and declarations of the party leadership evincing an ever-so-slight degree of independence in the conduct and formulation of international affairs seemed in 1957 to justify a modicum of optimism.

What remained a well-guarded secret for all except the policy-making Party élite, however, was the gravity of the Sino-Soviet conflict and the Rumanian Party's determination to exploit it to gain immunity from Soviet direction of Rumanian affairs. The Rumanian leadership had indeed discovered as early as December, 1956, that the Kremlin was unprepared to respect the political integrity of members of the bloc, enunciated unequivocally during the Hungarian crisis; rather, they intended to use the Hungarian revolution as an instrument for repudiation of all concessions wrested from Moscow since 1954. The Kremlin's rejection of Rumania's demands for limited economic independence and for the eventual withdrawal of Soviet military forces, submitted in December, 1956, reflected centralistic tendencies comparable to Stalin's. Whereas Stalinism was actually espoused by Gheorghiu-Dej and his associates in 1956 it had, in their view, to be legitimized by reaffirmation of the validity of the new principles governing relations among members of the bloc and the socialist camp in general, that is, equality among Stalinist communist states. The Kremlin's refusal to accept this doctrine, coupled with basic suspicion of Khrushchev's ultimate intentions toward Gheorghiu-Dej and his nationalist-Stalinist supporters, led to the strengthening of the Rumanians' bonds with China, whose basic attitude toward Khrushchev in the wake of the Hungarian uprising coincided with the Rumanians'.[9]

The validity of Gheorghiu-Dej's fears and suspicions was indeed confirmed in July, 1957, when Khrushchev's forces in Moscow defeated the Molotov-Bulganin "anti-Party" group, and the pro-Khrushchev forces in Rumania, headed by Miron Constantinescu, made a concurrent—but unsuccessful—challenge to the Rumanian Stalinists in power. These events caused Gheorghiu-Dej to consolidate his own forces against the threat of Khrushchevism and to accelerate Rumania's transformation into a nationalist-Stalinist "independent" communist state. A positive, if still camouflaged, independent course was in fact devised by November, 1957.

---

[9] On the intricate Sino-Rumanian relations consult Stephen Fischer-Galati, "Rumania and the Sino–Soviet Conflict," in *Eastern Europe in Transition,* ed. Kurt London (Baltimore, 1966), pp. 261–73.

Consensus on Present and Future Integration

It must be emphasized that the tendencies of the regime in 1957 were not based on any historic factors favoring or opposing integration, nor did they represent concessions to anti-Russian and pro-Western mass sentiments. The "autarchic" policies were formulated by the communist leadership exclusively in terms of its self-assigned *raison d'être*. Consolidation of power entailed the most rapid and efficient attainment of the goals of 1945, as restated at the Party Congress of 1955, and the reduction of obligatory dependence on the U.S.S.R. and the members of the Soviet bloc. Had the Soviet Union agreed to recognize Rumania's ambitions and to make the proper concessions, particularly in COMECON, the Rumanian regime would have espoused the principle and practice of close coordination within the bloc on economic, political, and cultural levels. However, Russia and the more advanced industrial nations of the bloc—most notably Czechoslovakia and East Germany—refused to accept the Rumanian views on "relations of the new type."

The anti-integrationist tendencies displayed by Rumania after 1957 have generally been ascribed to Rumania's dissatisfaction with COMECON policies. Rumanian opposition to being relegated to the position of producer of raw materials for the bloc, justified as it was in terms of Gheorghiu-Dej's plans, was in fact symptomatic only of Rumania's determination to resist restoration of Russian supremacy in Eastern Europe.[10]

[10] Consult, in particular, Gheorghiu-Dej's basic statement, "Situatia internationala si politica externa a Republicii Populare Romine" ("The International Situation and the Foreign Policy of the Rumanian People's Republic"), *Articole si cuvintari (august 1959–mai 1961)* ("Articles and Speeches, August 1959–May 1961") (Bucharest, 1961), pp. 208–29.

The very goal of rapid and multilateral industrialization expounded by the Rumanian regime was political, for only an industrially strong Rumania could exert leverage on Moscow for the acceptance of Gheorghiu-Dej's views on relations among members of the camp. It is also evident that Russia's resistance to Rumania's demands for greater recognition in COMECON and the Soviet formulas for multilateral industrialization were based on a correct assessment of Rumania's political aims. The political nature of the conflict became more evident in 1958, when the Rumanian regime expanded the scope of its international activities, both within the socialist camp and without, and pursued national communist policies at home, all in a manner disagreeable to the Kremlin.

The maintenance of friendly relations with Moscow's principal communist opponents, Yugoslavia and China, was rightly interpreted as Rumanian opposition to Khrushchev's views on socialist unity. Most offensive to Moscow was Gheorghiu-Dej's exploitation of Peking's resistance to Russian military domination of the socialist camp—which in the case of China resulted in refusal to join the Warsaw Pact, and in the case of Rumania resulted in the exertion of joint pressure with the Chinese for the withdrawal of Soviet troops from Rumania. The "voluntary" removal of the Soviet armies in the summer of 1958 presaged acceleration of Rumania's policy of disengagement from the Soviet bloc. The reinforcement of links with Western nations, most notably Germany and France, ostensibly in the pursuit of "peaceful coexistence," was explicitly designed to seek alternate avenues to industrialization. But the renewal of schemes for cooperation among Balkan nations, originally proposed by Georgi Dimitrov (and rejected by Stalin) in 1948 in the form of the Rumanian "Stoica Plan," was an assertion of Rumania's self-assigned place in the socialist camp and the international community in general as a force for the promotion of peace and friendly relations among all nations regardless of their socioeconomic and political order. These multilateral international activities, to which could be added official visits to nations of the *tiers monde* by Rumanian communist leaders, were ultimately designed to demonstrate Rumania's right of initiative in international affairs and her ability to pursue foreign policies based on principles formally approved by Moscow but denied to all satellites.[11]

The essentially anti-Russian character of these actions was emphasized by the pursuit of a ruthless Stalinist campaign at home directed against "revisionists" of all sorts, a euphemism for "Khrushchevites," "cosmopolitans," and all who in any way opposed Gheorghiu-Dej's plans for a Stalinist and socialist Rumania. The formal commitment to the construction of a Rumanian Socialist Republic *à la roumaine* was made at the Plenum of the Party in November, 1958.[12] That Plenum agreed on the need to strengthen the country's economy sufficiently to withstand external pressures and to consolidate the communists' power at home. It decided to accelerate the industrialization of the country as well as the socialization of agriculture and to secure such capital as might be needed for the attainment of its ambitious goals by increasing its trade with the West. It also decided to satisfy the economic requirements of the population at large by providing the masses with higher salaries, better prices for their

[11] A detailed analysis of these problems is contained in Fischer-Galati, *The New Rumania,* pp. 67 ff.

[12] The principal measures adopted at the Plenum and their significance were outlined in Gheorghiu-Dej's speech to that meeting published in *Scinteia,* December 2, 1958.

produce, improved housing, and, above all, a sense of participation in the construction of socialism in their own fatherland. The significance of these decisions became evident by 1960. At the Party's Third Congress in June, 1960, Gheorghiu-Dej was able to summarize the country's economic achievements and to outline future economic goals.[13] By then the rate of growth in industrial production was the fastest in Eastern Europe. In certain industries—chemical, mining, and building materials—production had virtually doubled in less than five years. The collectivization of agriculture was virtually complete. The pattern of foreign trade had changed significantly since 1958; though most of that trade was still with the Soviet Union and members of the bloc, the total volume and proportion of trade with Western Europe had nearly doubled. Most significant was the increase in trade with West Germany, which by 1960 exceeded Rumania's total trade with all socialist nations outside the Soviet bloc. The trade with West Germany and the *tiers monde* was actually one-third of Rumania's trade with all nations of Eastern Europe other than the U.S.S.R. Trade relations with France, the United Kingdom, and Italy had also shown remarkable progress; all in all, nearly 25 per cent of Rumania's total foreign trade was with the West. The doubling of all economic indices was sought for 1960–65; in certain areas of production, such as mining, electric power, and machine building, the rate of increase was to be even higher.

Nevertheless, until the spring of 1963 Rumania did not reject the possibility of remaining a faithful member of the Soviet bloc on compromise terms favorable to the Rumanians. To gain such terms, the Rumanian

[13] A detailed account of the Congress of 1960 may be found in Ionescu, *Communism in Rumania,* pp. 316 ff.

leadership relied mainly on the Sino-Soviet conflict and the consequential disunity of the socialist camp. In these years, too, the expression of Rumania's disaffection with Moscow's centralistic tendencies continued to focus on Rumania's position in COMECON —a position symbolic of the country's status in the Soviet bloc, the socialist community, and the international communist movement.

The basic Rumanian position vis-à-vis COMECON was recorded at the Third Party Congress in 1960 when Rumania was proclaimed to have reached a plateau of socialist development that entitled her to major stature in the Soviet bloc and in the socialist camp as a whole. The international policies of a prestigious industrial nation were bound to be different from those of "underdeveloped," pre-communist Rumania, and even from those of the pre-1960 party state. The country could now rightfully insist on observance of "relations of the new type" by all nations. The continuing rejection by Russia, Czechoslovakia, and East Germany of Rumania's claims, and their insistence on coordinated planning and assignment of responsibilities among member nations according to their natural resources and relative industrial development, precipitated the Rumanians' adoption of national and international policies of an increasingly independent character.

At home, the crucial development was the ever closer identification of the Rumanian historical tradition with the communist tradition, that is, the evolution of a doctrine of coincidence between the country's historic legacy and the communists' program for socialist construction. In sum, the communists claimed to be the executors of the country's historic goal: an independent, prosperous, and equalitarian Rumania.

This search for historic legitimacy, of total identification between the Rumanian Party and the Rumanian state, did not entail identification of "communist nationalism" with "bourgeois nationalism," nor did it entail identification of the bourgeois tradition with the revolutionary tradition until after Rumania's new independence was asserted in 1964. Neither was the role of the Party as unquestioned leading force in the country and in the process of socialist construction altered in any way. Authoritarianism, Stalinist in nature, remained the basic form of rule; democratic centralism was rejected as a principle unsuitable to Rumania's conditions. The Party was still being rebuilt in 1960 by the Rumanian Stalinists who had purged Miron Constantinescu's "Khrushchevites" from 1957 on. Its total membership was only 834,000—4.6 per cent of the country's total population—and the proportion of workers in the membership, less than half, but it was united behind Gheorghiu-Dej's plans for the development of communist Rumania.

Nevertheless, within the limits of political security —internal and external—required for the survival of the Gheorghiu-Dej regime, the budding communist nationalism was designed to secure a stronger base of domestic support for the execution of autarchic policies which the masses could identify as Rumanian and, in effect, anti-Russian. The intimate identification of the Party with the state was also necessary to allow the further development of economic relations with the noncommunist world for the fulfillment of the new *raison d'état*—the building of the Rumanian socialist state. Recognition of the validity of Rumania's goals by the forces favoring polycentrism would entail acceptance of the communists as rulers of a historic state and allow the pursuit of "mutually beneficial" relations among sovereign states on the basis of the principles of "peaceful coexistence." [14]

It must be recognized, however, that the communists' search for legitimacy and identification with the national historic tradition was far more cautious and gradual than the concurrent drive for equality among members of the socialist camp. At home it was limited to the exoneration and rehabilitation of progressive historic figures of the past and of "bourgeois" intellectuals and professional cadres ready to serve the country in the construction of socialism. The rewriting of Rumania's history began in 1960 and emphasized the contribution the Rumanian masses and their leaders had made to the attainment of national identity and social progress. An olive branch was extended to the intellectual community in the same year by increasing its representation in the Party, in recognition of its contribution to the country's socialist transformation. Universities and institutions of higher learning were gradually opened to individuals previously excluded because of improper social origin, and the general educational and professional requirements were made more stringent in an effort to raise the calibre of the "builders of socialism." By 1962 the educational and professional standards had reached levels of high competence, adequate for the constantly rising expectations of a rapidly developing industrial society. But intellectual and professional contacts with the West remained severely circumscribed. The historic tradition of close relations with Western Europe remained, in fact, limited to economic exchanges.

The international crises, focusing first on Berlin and later on Cuba, and the residual opposition to Ru-

[14] On these problems consult Fischer-Galati, *The New Rumania,* pp. 78 ff.

manian Stalinism by the Rumanian masses, favored
reliance on the Chinese lever in the years antedating
the Cuban crisis. Certainly after the issuance of the
Moscow Declaration of 1960, the Rumanian communists echoed the Chinese positions relative to the conditions for unity of the socialist camp and the role of
member states, even if only to the extent to which
Peking's views coincided with Bucharest's and did not
directly affront the Kremlin. Nevertheless, the expected price of Rumania's moderation in the Sino-
Soviet conflict was Russian adherence to Rumania's
demands for equality in the camp, bloc, and COME-
CON. As "persuasion" appeared futile, the Rumanians
seized on the "humiliation" of the Soviet giant in the
Cuban crisis (and consequent need for accommodation
with the United States), and on the consequent exacer-
bation of the Sino-Soviet conflict, to force acceptance
by Moscow of Gheorghiu-Dej's terms for unity of the
bloc and of the socialist camp. The original expression
of Rumania's rejection of Russian domination of the
bloc and camp was *pro forma* limited to COMECON
and issued in that context in March, 1963. The rejection of Russia's hegemony in the bloc and leadership of the camp, and the statement of Rumanian independence, were made public in April, 1964.[15]

The character of Rumania's opposition to Soviet
hegemony as expressed in the 1963 and 1964 statements
reflected the irreconcilability of the Sino-Soviet conflict. In the spring and summer of 1963 the Rumanian
leadership sought to secure independence from the
COMECON prescriptions for economic development
and cooperation (which it rejected in March, 1963)
through intensification of friendly relations with
China. Economic pressure by Russia and her faithful

[15] *Statement of the Rumanian Workers' Party,* pp. 269 ff.

allies, combined with China's inability to provide viable economic alternatives, forced the Rumanian regime to veer more and more toward the West later in that year and to seek unequivocal recognition of the communist regime's legitimacy abroad and at home. The preferred solution for the maintenance of independence remained, however, the securing of general international acceptance of Rumania's views on the equality of all members of the camp and of their right to pursue national policies compatible with their national interests. The growing threat of polarization of the communist camp into Chinese and Russian blocs, with resultant weakening of Rumania's chances to maintain her independence among pro-Soviet neighbors, precipitated the adoption of a neutral attitude in the Sino-Soviet conflict. In fact, in the fall of 1963 the Rumanian communists assumed the role of mediators in the Sino-Soviet conflict as self-styled champions of the unity of the socialist camp. The failure of their mediation efforts, recorded in both Peking's and Moscow's February, 1964, rejection of the compromise proposed by the Rumanian "honest brokers," forced readjustments in the Rumanians' plans of how best to maintain their independence from Moscow. This was because the attempted mediation involved intra-Party as well as intra-state problems.

The Chinese opposition to Moscow in 1964 focused on ideological differences as well as on territorial problems. Territorial revisionism relative to Mongolia and other Soviet possessions in the Far East was placed by Mao Tse-tung in the context of illegal seizure of territory by the Soviet Union elsewhere, including Bessarabia and northern Bukovina, wrested from Rumania in 1940 and not restituted after World War II. Potentially this Chinese revisionism—so dear to Rumanian "bourgeois nationalists" but until that time studiously side-stepped by Rumanian "communist nationalists"—was one more bond beyond the established one of opposition to Soviet domination of the camp. But the Chinese failure to offer reasonable terms for a possible solution of their conflict with the Russians while raising issues so offensive to the Soviet Union placed the Rumanian "mediators" in a precarious position. In March, 1964, Khrushchev appeared determined to excommunicate the adamant Chinese from the socialist camp, to re-establish Soviet leadership in the socialist community of nations, and, in any case, to restore Soviet hegemony in the bloc. Rumanian independence at both the Party and state levels had to be arrested, if not altogether terminated. This threat forced the Rumanian leadership to issue the celebrated "Statement on the Stand of the Rumanian Workers' Party Concerning the Problem of the International Communist and Working-Class Movement" in April, 1964, which outlined the fundamental Rumanian views on international relations in general and relations within the communist camp in particular. The statement has become the fundamental law of Rumanian "national communism," currently a principal force of disintegration of the Soviet bloc, of the unity of the international "socialist movement," and of the socialist camp as a whole.[16]

[16] On the significance of the *Statement* consult Fischer-Galati, *The New Rumania,* pp. 99 ff.

5: THE PRESENT STAGE

Inter-camp Relations

The matter of international cooperation, and integration with members of the socialist camp, was spelled out in the lengthy statement of the Rumanian Workers' Party. The fundamental principles contained in the statement, if fully implemented, would indeed have led—as in fact they did by March, 1968 —to the "independent" communist Rumania of today. The statement's basic thesis is the right of all communist and workers' parties and of socialist states to "elaborate, choose, or change the forms and methods of socialist construction" in accordance with the "concrete historic conditions prevailing in their own countries. . . ." To secure these rights, it was further stipulated that "bearing in mind the diversity of the conditions of socialist construction, there are not nor can there be any unique patterns or recipes; no one can decide what is and what is not correct for other countries and parties. It is up to every Marxist-Leninist Party, it is a sovereign right to each socialist state, to elaborate, choose or change the forms and methods of socialist construction. The strict observance of the basic principles of the new-type relations among the socialist countries is the primary prerequisite of the unity and cohesion of these countries and of the world socialist system performing its decisive role in the development of mankind." [1]

These principles were clearly aimed at protecting the country's and the Party's integrity against "interference in internal affairs" by the Soviet Union. Specific protective clauses were also included. The Rumanians stated their unshakable allegiance to the principle of the unity of the socialist camp of equals, thus endorsing the Chinese views on the subject. They also restated their determination to develop "relations of cooperation with countries which have a different social-political system, on the basis of the principles of peaceful coexistence." For the Rumanians, these principles were equated with the "development of trade, of economic relations based on mutual advantage, as well as the extension of technical and scientific links, of cultural exchanges . . ." that would improve the "international climate" and "strengthen peace throughout the world."

The most specific demands voiced by the Rumanians were for the abolition of all military blocs (including the Warsaw Pact), the conclusion of a German peace treaty (with implied recognition of the political existence and legitimacy of West Germany), and the enlargement of the membership of COMECON to include all members of the socialist camp acting in accordance with the principles of equality of members and the "most flexible forms and methods of cooperation." Offensive as these views were to the Soviet Union, they naturally added to the existing friction between the dissident Rumanians and Russia and the loyal members of the Soviet bloc. In fact, the statement was a declaration of war against Soviet domination of

[1] *Statement of the Rumanian Workers' Party,* pp. 286–87.

the bloc inasmuch as the Kremlin had declared itself opposed to accepting the validity of even less specific conditions for Rumanian "independence."

The subsequent evolution of Rumanian relations with the Soviet Union, the members of the bloc, and the socialist camp, at both the Party and state levels, and with noncommunist states—in other words the evolution of Rumania's anti-integrationist policies— have reflected the Party's awareness of the impossibility of meaningful reconciliation of Russia's centralistic orientation and Rumania's political interests. The "Rumanian course" has also reflected the dilemmas and contradictions inherent in seeking ill-assorted crutches for support against Russian "imperialism" at home and abroad. The principle of the unity of the socialist camp—a euphemism for the maintenance of the split caused by the Sino-Soviet conflict—was even as early as 1964 in obvious contradiction to the policy of economic and political coexistence with the arch-enemy of the Chinese wing, the American "imperialists." And these contradictions were deepened by such subsequent actions as befriending West Germany and Israel, the sworn enemies of members of the Soviet bloc and of the Arab communist parties. In Rumania proper, the drive to secure acceptance of the Party's historic claims of fulfilling the independent traditions of the Rumanians unleashed the latent forces of nationalism, cultural in form but political in purpose. These contradictions have placed the Rumanian leaders in an ideologically indefensible and politically dangerous position, and have determined the unique character of communist Rumania and of her present relations with the members of the Communist party states.[2]

[2] A brief analytical statement is contained in Fischer-Galati, *The New Rumania*, pp. 104 ff.

The direct political conflict—inherent in the struggle for independence from Soviet domination—has been with the Russian Communist Party and state. The Rumanians' uncompromising position, in its original formulation of April, 1964, was held until the death of Gheorghiu-Dej in March, 1965. However, even during that period of comparative moderation, the Rumanian regime pursued policies designed to consolidate its independence on bases different from those stated in 1964. Most significant was the gradual rekindling of nationalism—with an anti-Russian character—focusing on the Bessarabian question. It is uncertain whether the Rumanians' territorial revisionism —made public in December, 1964—was a deliberate reassertion of Rumania's independence at a time when the Brezhnev and Kosygin partnership replaced Khrushchev, or a response to a continuing Soviet pressure to force Rumania back into line. The Russian methods of coercion through economic pressure, reopening of the Transylvanian question, and insistence on reasserting Soviet supremacy in the camp were at work in the fall of 1964. In any event, to the Rumanian leadership, the formal reopening of the Bessarabian issue was designed to gain the support of the Rumanian people for anti-Russian activities unrelated to "proletarian internationalism." The appeal to nationalism grew stronger in 1965 when blatantly nationalist theses were expounded in official reinterpretation of Rumanian history and Russo-Rumanian relations. The Russians were once again historical "villains," and their contribution to the "liberation" of Rumania in August, 1944, was minimized.[3] The Rumanian communist

[3] Most striking was the publication of Marx's critical notes on tsarist imperialism by A. Otetea and S. Schwann in December, 1964. Karl Marx, *Insemnari despre romani* ("Notes Concerning the Rumanians") (Bucharest, 1964).

leaders were now the primary architects of the "armed uprising," executed with the "assistance" of the Soviet armed forces. The Rumanians' defiance of Russia— or defense against Russian pressures—had become even more pronounced by July, 1965, when the April, 1964, formulas were revised in the direction of greater independence at both the state and Party levels. The Party shed the compromise appellation of "Rumanian Workers' Party" in favor of "Rumanian Communist Party," to correspond to the self-declared elevation of Rumania from the status of People's Democracy to Socialist Republic.[4] The equalization in rank of both the Party and the state to that of the most "advanced" members of the Soviet bloc—the U.S.S.R. and Czechoslovakia—was offensive enough to Russia, but the preference for "Socialist Republic of Romania" (emphasized by the readoption of the historical Latin-derived spelling which had been abandoned in 1954) rather than the "Rumanian Socialist Republic," added insult to injury. Since the summer of 1965, the Rumanian leadership has grown increasingly bolder in deepening its independence from Moscow. The territorial claims to Bessarabia and northern Bukovina, though somewhat soft-pedaled through restatement of the inviolability of the frontiers drawn in Europe by the peace settlements of World War II, have not actually been renounced. The demands for liquidation of the Warsaw Pact, concurrently with NATO, assumed more strident tones after the unequivocal spelling out of that anti-Russian position by Nicolae Ceausescu in May, 1966. The Rumanians' rejection of their military partners' views on nonproliferation of atomic weapons in March, 1968, is only the latest evidence of

[4] On these matters consult the far-reaching speech by Nicolae Ceausescu, *Report to the Ninth Congress of the Rumanian Communist Party* (Bucharest, 1965), pp. 5–101.

Ceausescu's determination not to allow the Russians to obtain any legal means for coercion of weaker socialist states by virtue of superior military power.

In its most spectacular form, however, the Rumanians' independent course has manifested itself in the constant opposition to the restoration of Soviet hegemony in the socialist camp. The Rumanians have opposed all Russian attempts to restore the unity of the camp through action by an international communist conference. They dramatized this determination by walking out of the February, 1968, meeting of communist parties held in Budapest, when the assembled parties were veering in the direction of supporting Soviet positions vis-à-vis the Chinese and other dissidents. The walk-out was also an expression of Rumanian resistance to Russian reaction against Rumanian policies unrelated to the international communist movement. The Rumanian Party's decision to maintain friendly relations with the Communist Party of Israel, and of the Rumanian state with the state of Israel during and after the Arab–Israeli war of June, 1967—motivated by economic and political factors other than those of the Soviet Union and the Russian Party—clashed directly with that of the members of the Soviet bloc and the Arab parties and states. The denunciation of Rumania's "treasonable" policies toward Israel, made by the Syrian delegation at Budapest—clearly with Russia's consent, if not at Moscow's behest—was the ostensible reason for the Rumanians' exodus from that meeting. The Syrian and Russian moves in Budapest underline the depth of the Russo-Rumanian conflict, and the extent of Russia's displeasure with Rumanian's independent course.[5]

[5] On these problems consult the "Decision of the Central Committee of the Rumania Communist Party" of March 1, 1968, published in *Scinteia,* March 2, 1968.

The Rumanian doctrine of the supremacy of the
national interest is insufferable to the Kremlin. The
Russians have repeatedly expressed their irritation
over Rumanian actions, justified in terms of national
as against international communist interests. Rumania's establishing normal diplomatic relations with
West Germany in 1967, over the protests of East Germany and without Moscow's consent, was an act of
overt defiance. Almost as offensive was her refusal to
join the Soviet bloc in condemning Israel, and the
subsequent expansion of the scope of Israeli–Rumanian economic and cultural relations. Rumania's rapprochement with West Germany and her independent
attitude toward Israel were caused primarily by her
desire to secure markets and capital for the country's
economic development, in order to lessen her economic
dependence on the Soviet Union and the Soviet bloc.
Nevertheless, none of Rumania's actions—at the Party
or state levels—have affected vital Russian national
interests sufficiently to warrant more forcible Russian
"interference in Rumanian affairs." It is most unlikely
that the Rumanian leadership would risk a direct confrontation with Moscow and thus, at least on the surface, "friendly, comradely relations" are maintained
between the two countries. In reality, of course, the
conflict is acute, and the opposing positions are at
present irreconcilable. This situation has constantly
affected, if not determined, the nature of the relations
between Rumania and the Rumanian Party and other
members of the bloc and socialist camp.

The most direct impact was on relations with Hungary. It has been assumed that until 1964 Rumania's
relations with Hungary, at the state and Party levels,
have been correct if not necessarily cordial. The chau-
vinist manifestations displayed by part of the Magyar

population of Transylvania—most notably university students—during the revolt of 1956 were officially condemned by Budapest. Nevertheless, the Rumanian regime took steps to curtail the cultural autonomy of the Hungarians in Transylvania after the revolt, ostensibly because these manifestations were reflections of "bourgeois" ideological influences which had to be eradicated. With the degeneration of Russo-Rumanian relations, and particularly after the reopening of territorial questions in 1964, the process of making Transylvania more "Rumanian" gained momentum. The Rumanian action was motivated in part by the need to gain mass support for causes identified with the Rumanian historic tradition (among which anti-Magyar sentiment occupied a paramount place), but mostly because of the Russian encouragement of Hungarian irredentism and the accompanying threat of redrawing Transylvania's frontiers on the basis of ethnic-territorial factors.

Whether the Russian pressure exerted on dissident Rumania through reopening of the Transylvanian question was a reflection of official Hungarian revisionism or an independent political action of the Kremlin in which Budapest tacitly concurred is uncertain. In any case the Russian action and Rumanian reaction, or counteraction, has once again focused attention on territorial and nationality questions in Rumanian-Hungarian relations, to the detriment of the further development of economic and cultural ties. Perhaps, paradoxically, the Hungarians did not share the Russian, Czechoslovak, and East German anti-Rumanian positions in COMECON and are still cooperative with the Rumanians in economic affairs. But cultural exchanges have declined and, in general, relations between the two countries have become formal and somewhat rigid. At the Party level, the Hungarians have adhered more closely to the Russian ideological positions than they have to Russia's political and economic line at the state level. The Hungarian Party has favored the convening of conferences designed to re-establish Russia's domination of the camp and has sided with Russia in all ideological disputes with the Rumanians. Most striking was the Hungarian criticism of the Rumanian walkout at the Budapest conference, and the wholehearted support given to Moscow's call for another, formal conference of all communist parties to implement the Kremlin's demands for ideological conformity so opposed to the Rumanians. Evidently, relations between Hungary and Rumania are likely to be more strained than before, with as yet unpredictable consequences for the unity of the bloc and the camp.

Rumania's relations with Bulgaria are ambiguous also. Since 1957 the Rumanians have been seeking close ties with a view to implementing the Stoica Plan for Balkan federation. As Russo-Rumanian relations deteriorated, Rumania's courting of Bulgaria became more intensive. Ceausescu, in particular, has tried, mostly unsuccessfully, to reduce Bulgaria's subservience to Russia and to encourage manifestations of independence at least to the extent of accepting the Stoica Plan and strengthening regional autonomy. The Bulgarians' evinced interest in participating in the Rumanian scheme for creating a "zone of peace" in the Balkans, and the related outward manifestations of "fraternal solidarity" have not satisfied Bucharest. Sofia's continuing subservience to Moscow in political and ideological matters, as evidenced by total endorsement of all Russian schemes and proposals no matter how opposed to Rumanian positions, has proven the futility of Rumanian efforts to convert the Bulgarians to a more flexible—if not necessarily Rumanian—line.

Rumania's ties with East Germany are less ambiguous—in fact, they verge on hostility—as do her ties with Poland, which reflect Bucharest's rapprochement with Bonn. The East Germans have been the primary supporters of Russian positions on economic integration under COMECON, both before and after the Rumanian denunciation of those policies in March, 1963, and they have expressed profound displeasure over all aspects of Rumanian foreign relations. The East German attitude is derived primarily from its total dependence on Moscow for political survival; however, in no small measure the East Germans regard the Rumanians as upstarts and traditional inferiors, at both the state and Party levels. The Rumanian reaction to Ulbricht's positions has been equally negative, with the result that only the most perfunctory bilateral relations are maintained between the two parties and states.

More significant is the deterioration of Rumania's relations with Poland, which had been closer, traditionally, than those between Rumania and East Germany. In 1956 the Rumanians were flirting with Gomulka when Polish assertions of independence coincided with Rumanian views on the relationship among members of the bloc and camp, at the same time opposing the internal liberalization policies of the Poles as anti-Stalinist. Gradually, as Gomulka's liberalism and independent policies waned, with corresponding realignment with Russian positions, and the Rumanians became closer to the Poles of 1956, friction began to develop. The Poles now regard the Rumanians as a destructive force sabotaging integration and the common interests of the Soviet bloc and socialist camp. Gomulka is totally identified with Moscow on matters related to Germany, China, and Rumania; and Ceausescu is apparently more contemptuous than resentful toward Gomulka's attitudes. In any event, relations between the two countries and parties are static and rigid with no immediate likelihood of improvement.

Similar rigidity had been characteristic of Rumanian-Czechoslovak relations until the removal of Novotny from power in January, 1968. Novotny's dependence on Moscow and his support of all Russian positions in international affairs was as offensive to the Rumanians as the scarcely hidden Czechoslovak contempt for Rumania's demands for economic equality with the more advanced socialist nations and its ostentatious assumption of the title Socialist Republic, which was, until 1965, the distinguishing mark of Czechoslovakia with respect to the "underdeveloped" members of the Soviet bloc. The assumption of power by the "reformist" group headed by Alexander Dubcek brought about closer relations between Czechoslovakia and Rumania. As early as February, 1968, the Rumanian power élite paid homage to Dubcek and to the Czechoslovak independent course in a state visit to Prague. And during the confrontation between the Czechoslovak and the Russian and "conservative" allied parties of Poland, East Germany, Hungary, and Bulgaria in July, 1968, the Rumanians sided openly with the Czechs. After the threat of Soviet military intervention appeared to have subsided in early August, the Rumanian power élite returned to Czechoslovakia to conclude a far-reaching treaty of friendship and mutual assistance with Czechoslovakia and to reiterate its support for the right of all nations to work out their own policies, without interference, on the basis of "objective historical conditions." And even after the Soviet invasion

of Czechoslovakia on August 20–21, Rumania vocifer-
ously reiterated its support for Czechoslovakia's right
to political self-determination.

It has been suggested that prior to the invasion
Rumania's stand—which coincided with that of Yugoslavia—was partly motivated by a common desire to
strengthen the political and economic bonds among
the "dissidents" in Eastern Europe. In fact, the historic
antecedents of the interwar Little Entente came to the
minds of political analysts of Eastern Europe. In any
event, for Rumania, as well as for Czechoslovakia and
even for Yugoslavia, the rapprochement of the summer
of 1968 was also designed to reduce their isolation from
the rest of the Soviet bloc and provide a common front
against pressures exerted by the conservative members
of the East European party states. This was particularly
true of Rumania, which has not been consulted on any
important issues affecting the bloc since the meeting
of the Warsaw Pact in March, 1968, and has been, in
effect, ostracized from the bloc as a sign of Moscow's
growing displeasure with Ceausescu's independence.
Indeed, Rumania has become essentially isolated from
all members of the Soviet bloc except Czechoslovakia,
none of which are subscribing to Bucharest's views on
the relations among members of the bloc when such
views are contrary to those of the Soviet Union.[6] Nevertheless, the Rumanian independent course has not
brought about the disintegration of the bloc or, for
that matter, of political, cultural, and economic organizations in which only members of the bloc are
represented. Rumania is still a member of COMECON

[6] The essence of Rumania's position vis-à-vis Czechoslovakia
and the Czechoslovak crisis is contained in the "Declaration of
the Grand National Assembly of the Socialist Republic of Rumania Regarding the Fundamental Principles of Rumania's
Foreign Policy," published in *Scinteia*, August 23, 1968.

and of the Warsaw Pact, although the Rumanian actions have weakened the cohesion of these organizations. In that respect, Rumania's position is entirely different from that of ex-members of the Soviet bloc, Albania and Yugoslavia, whose own independent course has resulted in their abandonment of collective commitments and programs.

Rumania's decision to retain her commitments to the bloc are consonant with her national interests. The Rumanian economy is still heavily dependent on relations with members of the bloc, most notably the Soviet Union. The Soviet-Rumanian trade protocol for 1968 envisages a volume of 770 million rubles, or slightly over 25 per cent of the total Rumanian foreign trade for that year. Even if the proportion of Russo-Rumanian trade has dropped increasingly in recent years (7.3 per cent in the share of Rumania's total 1966 foreign trade, 17.4 per cent in 1963, and about 25.6 per cent in 1958), Rumanian trade with Russia is essential for the attainment of Rumania's economic goals.[7] The comparable decline in Rumanian trade relations with the other members of COMECON has been less significant because it was more than compensated for by the constant increase of trade with Western Europe. Her geographic position also precludes the pursuit of policies that could be regarded as fully incompatible with the national interests of the Soviet Union and other members of the bloc. Thus, withdrawal from COMECON or the Warsaw Pact, or energetic pressing of demands for revision of the postwar frontiers of the member nations of the bloc are unlikely to occur. The Rumanian dilemma, caused by realistic economic and geopolitical considerations, is

[7] Important statistical information may be found in *East Europe,* Vol. 17, no. 9 (September, 1968), pp. 51–52.

also translated in her championing of the principles of the unity of the socialist camp and her unique relations with members of the camp, as different from the bloc. Theoretically, the bloc is subordinated to the camp; practically, the camp of equals constitutes a protective defense against pressures by a bloc of satellites.

It is for such pragmatic reasons that the Rumanians have maintained correct, often even friendly, relations with the communist nation states not belonging to the Soviet bloc. The specific character of the relations has been determined by differing "national" requirements, invariably political but occasionally reflecting broader economic interests of the state. These considerations account for the diversity of relations with communist states at opposite poles of the communist ideological and political spectra. Of greatest significance for this study are Rumania's relations with China and the neutrals of the communist left and right, North Korea and North Vietnam and Yugoslavia, respectively.

Rumania's relations with China most accurately reflect the dilemmas, paradoxes, and complexities of her independent course.[8] The mutual utilization, by China and Rumania, of common opposition to Soviet centralism and internationalism for furthering their own independent, nationalist courses lost much of its effectiveness in 1965 when the Rumanians veered to the right and the Chinese to the left. Chou En-lai's visit to Rumania that year showed Ceausescu and his close associates that the Chinese demanded total adherence to their line as the price of active support of Rumania's "deviationism." Mao's "cultural revolution" further alienated China from Rumania, both doctrinally and in terms of possibilities for effective joint pressure

[8] Details in Fischer-Galati, *Rumania and the Sino-Soviet Conflict*, pp. 261 ff.

against Moscow. The rather extensive trade that had been developing between the two countries in the late fifties and early sixties was cut back from approximately 5 per cent of Rumania's total trade in 1959 to only half that percentage in 1968. Nevertheless, the Chinese have avoided any and all polemics toward the Rumanians and have supported Bucharest's positions on the unity of the camp. However, the Chinese are no longer actively supporting Rumanian deviationism; nor are they using the Rumanians as spokesmen for anti-Soviet positions. Rather, it is the Rumanians who cling to China, at least to the extent to which Rumanian interests coincide with Peking's. The Rumanians' insistence on avoidance of condemnation of the Chinese party at the Budapest conference of February, 1968, was a Rumanian initiative; the coincidence between the Rumanian and Chinese positions on atomic controls stems from similarity of national interests rather than advance coordination of common policies.

The gradual loss of leverage—evident at least since the summer of 1967—has forced the Rumanians to adjust their relations with several members of the camp. If the Chinese position is still regarded as sufficiently strong to oppose Moscow's quest for hegemony within the camp, it has had to be reinforced, certainly since the summer of 1967, through the re-establishment of Rumania's position as a neutral and potential leader of a third force in the international communist movement. The third-force concept first emerged in 1963 but was shelved during the early stages of the Vietnamese war when the unity of the camp against imperialist aggression had to be proclaimed.[9] It remained in mothballs until 1967, when the "cultural revolution" had shattered all possibility of maintaining even *pro forma*

[9] Fischer-Galati, *The New Rumania,* pp. 93 ff.

unity, and in effect resulted in growing polycentrism in what was believed to be an essentially monolithic Chinese bloc. The differences between the Chinese and Russian views on formulas for settlement of the Vietnamese war helped Rumania's position of independence from Moscow as long as Hanoi's views veered toward Peking's. However, even in 1965 and 1966, the Rumanians exploited their independence and "friendship" with China for soundings of Peking's and Hanoi's inclinations for a compromise solution. In 1967, the last of their soundings fully revealed the weakness of their bargaining power as "friends" of China and the need to revert to the position of third force in the camp. Peking's blunt rejection of Rumanian efforts to persuade the Chinese to agree to a compromise formula for re-establishing peace in Vietnam on terms acceptable to Hanoi (and Washington), which occurred at the time of a Rumanian state visit to China in June, 1967, resulted in the Rumanians strengthening their bilateral relations with fellow "neutrals" in the Far East, most notably North Vietnam and North Korea, and in similar intensification of bilateral contacts with neutral nonruling communist parties.

Rumania had entertained close relations with North Korea since 1958 when the Rumanians cited the example of Chinese troop withdrawals from that country as a precedent for withdrawal of foreign troops from all fraternal communist countries. But North Korea's geographic remoteness, and her poverty, limited contacts to cultural exchanges and Rumanian statements of support for North Korean policies in the Far East, particularly vis-à-vis "American imperialism." In February, 1968, however, the Rumanians went beyond their traditional support of North Korea by endorsing not only the correctness of Pyongyang's policies in the

Pueblo incident but also the "independent"—in this case "neutral"—course in the Sino-Soviet conflict, while stressing the similarities between Rumanian and North Korean views of intracamp and international affairs. The Rumanians took it upon themselves, probably with Pyongyang's consent, to speak for the "absent fraternal parties," which included the North Korean, at the Budapest meeting and to justify the ideological and political correctness of the Korean decision not to attend.

Rumania's relations with North Vietnam have been less well defined than those with North Korea. Before the Vietnamese war they were generally limited to formal exchanges of greetings and Rumanian endorsement of Hanoi's struggle for liberation and national unification of the Vietnamese people.[10] The internationalization of the Vietnamese "war of liberation" through active American intervention placed Bucharest in the difficult position of potential mediator between the United States—whose support it needed for pursuit of its own policies of independence from the Soviet Union—and North Vietnam—a small communist state whose national interests were frustrated by the United States.

As the Rumanians have been the greatest defenders of the rights of the small national state against acceptance of the will of "imperialistic" giants, the North Vietnamese were the first to question the sincerity of the Rumanians' dedication to their own views on the unity of the camp. The endorsement by the Rumanians of mutually accusing slogans devised by Peking and

[10] A summary statement of Rumanian positions vis-à-vis North Vietnam is contained in the "Declaration of the Government of the Socialist Republic of Rumania Regarding the Situation in Vietnam," which appeared in *Scinteia* April 6, 1968.

Moscow that only restoration of the unity of the camp could bring common communist action against the American imperialist aggressor—without, however, indicating whose slogan they were in fact endorsing—allowed Bucharest to pursue its ambiguous policies toward Moscow, Peking, Washington, and Hanoi. Attempts at mediation could be and have been conducted in all ideological and political capacities, the latest in that of the "third force" in the socialist camp and champion of international peace. Whether Hanoi accepts Bucharest's "neutral" posture at face value and regards the Rumanians as true brethren in the socialist camp is uncertain. In practical terms, North Vietnam has rejected the Rumanian efforts and has carefully avoided drawing similarities between the Rumanians' independence and their own. Certainly, neither Rumania nor North Vietnam has done much to strengthen the "unity of the camp," and both are using that slogan for the attainment of their own national interests. In that respect there is coincidence between Rumanian and Vietnamese independence and neutrality. There is also some coincidence between the Rumanian and the Vietnamese parties' wooing the "neutral" non-ruling communist parties. The Rumanian intensification of receptions for, and statements of common principles issued by, representatives of such parties visiting Rumania coincides, perhaps accidentally, with similar Vietnamese efforts. But as they all stress the principles of unity of the camp and anti-imperialism, it is difficult necessarily to equate the Vietnamese with the Rumanian positions. In the case of the Rumanians there can be little doubt that the wining and dining of representatives of fraternal parties with like sentiments is to gain support for Rumanian views on relations among communist parties and states and, whenever possible, recognition of Rumania's leadership of the neutrals.

The neutralist stand, but even more so the posture of fellow independents, has governed Rumania's relations with Yugoslavia. These relations, like those with China, have posed serious dilemmas for Bucharest because the Yugoslavs could provide little leverage for the Rumanian struggle for independence, certainly not enough to justify Rumania's emulation of the Yugoslav formula for independence. Titoism has been suspect to the Rumanians because of its "liberalism" and its unorthodox economic policies; and Rumania's independence, in turn, was looked upon with mistrust and later jealousy by Belgrade. As late as the summer of 1964, Tito tried to dissuade the Rumanians from pursuing an independent course too offensive to Moscow, presumably because he had pre-empted the position himself. As the Rumanians moved ahead of their own accord and by their own formulas, they began to compete with Yugoslavia for the favors of the West and invaded the previous Yugoslav sphere of influence among the *tiers monde,* with substantial success.

Undoubtedly, the Yugoslav adherence to the policies of the Soviet bloc in the Arab–Israeli war—from which the Rumanians alone deviated—was partly motivated by the gradual displacement of Yugoslav influence in the Middle East by aggressive Rumanian economic penetration. Cooperation with the Rumanians has been largely limited to economic matters of mutual national benefit such as the so-called Iron Gates project for developing hydroelectric power through harnessing and exploiting the potential of the Danube. Ideological consultations on matters related to Soviet "imperialism" within the socialist camp have been held periodically since 1964 and frequently since 1967, with both Rumanians and Yugoslavs anxious to maintain the validity of their common doctrine of equality of members in the socialist camp. But there has been no emulation by the Rumanians of the Yugoslav internal policies, and few meaningful contacts between Yugoslav liberals and Rumanian conservatives in the intellectual and technical areas.

Common independence, if not necessarily neutrality, is the basic tie linking Rumania with Cuba and Albania. Relations with Albania, which in 1964 were designed to impress Moscow with Bucharest's independence and the possibility of Rumania's following in the Albanians' footsteps, have become less important as Rumania's independence became a fact. Relations are correct but insignificant. Relations with Cuba have been strained because of Cuba's refusal to identify its own independent course with that of Rumania and because of Havana's refusal to refrain from implicit (occasionally explicit) condemnation of Rumania's flirtation with the archenemy, America. The Rumanians and the Cubans nevertheless share enough common problems—most notably proximity to hostile superpowers and the fear of a compromise between the United States and Russia—to voice common opposition to Soviet moves for re-establishment of unity of the camp *à la russe*.

The complexity of Rumania's relations, forced upon her by the need to protect the interests of the Party and the related independent course, has not resulted in the consolidation of her position within the bloc or the camp. In fact, the Rumanians are aware of their isolation, most painfully since their solo exit from the

Budapest conference in February and the Czechoslovak crisis of August, 1968.

Relations Outside the Socialist Camp

Rumania's attempt to ensure her independence through relations outside the socialist camp has not provided a clear-cut solution to her problems. In accordance with her principle of international cooperation with all nations, regardless of their socioeconomic and political structures, she has indeed been most active in supporting cooperative international activities whenever possible. The Rumanians have frequently deviated from the Soviet bloc and from other members of the socialist camp in supporting broad international decisions by the United Nations. They have worked for the strengthening of that organization in all aspects of its activities and, symbolically, the General Assembly's president for 1967–68 was the Rumanian Minister of Foreign Affairs, Corneliu Manescu. Rumania has also evinced interest in some form of auxiliary membership in the Common Market and has been an ardent exponent of the integration of the European community of nations for the benefit of Europe as a whole. On a regional basis, she has steadfastly advanced the Stoica Plan for Balkan unity and multilateral cooperation.

These attempts are, however, unproductive by their very nature. They are ideologically suspect because they entail direct or indirect collaboration with the main enemies of the socialist community—the "American imperialists," "German revisionists," and "Israeli Zionists." Ideological considerations aside—though a close rapprochement with these "hostile elements" may weaken the Rumanian communists' position at home and within the socialist camp—the current international political and financial crises are not conducive to realization of Rumania's economic and political interests in a manner that would assure her true independence from the Soviet bloc. The United States, for example, has not yet rescinded the discriminatory tariffs applicable to members of the communist camp, despite repeated demands for granting Rumania favored-nation treatment. West Germany, Rumania's most active Western trading partner, is branded as an aggressor by the Soviet Union and its conservative partners in the bloc, a fact which forces caution upon both Bonn and Bucharest.[11] France, despite the steady consolidation of traditional, cultural, and even economic ties, and a state visit by De Gaulle in May, 1968, has carefully avoided long-range commitments, as has "neutral" Rumania. And ties with India, Pakistan, or Iran have not brought meaningful economic benefits to Bucharest.

Thus, in the constant process of evaluation of, and adjustment to, the realities of the international situation and the "objective Rumanian conditions," the Rumanians have chosen as their slogan, "By ourselves." This slogan, borrowed from the National Liberals of the twenties, reveals the need for flexibility and adjustment and in the last analysis for a total national commitment to independence. How feasible is that formula in the late sixties? How successful will the Rumanians

[11] The extraordinary increase in Rumania's trade with West Germany—which quadrupled in less than eight years—is likely to diminish as a result of the Czechoslovak crisis and Soviet denunciations of West Germany and of Rumania's too-friendly ties with Bonn.

be in attaining their goals by themselves? And at what cost?

The viability of the Rumanian formulas for integration and community building within the family of communist party states will be determined by the degree of national commitment to the purposes of the Rumanian Communist Party and state, the country's economic development, and the evolution of international relations both within and without the socialist camp.

Geographic and Demographic Factors

The Rumanian doctrinal positions on international cooperation presuppose that the construction of socialism in a free and independent Rumania represents the supreme desire of all her inhabitants. It recognizes the significance of geographic factors to the extent that the country's proximity to the U.S.S.R., as well as its geographic location within the Soviet bloc, renders Rumania vulnerable to Soviet pressures, political, economic, and even military. These factors limit Rumania's freedom of action, forcing certain compromises in the formulation of Rumanian policies. Were Rumania's geographic location different, it is quite probable that her independence would have been proclaimed sooner and her disengagement from the Soviet bloc would have been at least as complete as Yugoslavia's. Rumanian spokesmen have repeatedly emphasized the significance of these factors and have tended to justify their cautious approach to external problems on the risks inherent in proximity to the

"Russian bear." [12] More significantly, they have justified their "conservative" internal policies on the same grounds. However, short of military intervention or total economic isolation, the Soviet Union cannot remove the present leadership from power. There are no pro-Soviet groups in the Rumanian Party or society at large that could be used by the Kremlin for subverting the regime. The Russians have encouraged the Hungarian minority to seek closer ties with Hungary—a more trustworthy Soviet partner than Rumania—with a view to reopening the Transylvanian question, but apparently with limited success. There is no evidence that the Hungarians of Transylvania prefer Hungarian communism to Rumanian, although many are dissatisfied with the growing anti-Magyar nationalism manifest in Transylvania. The Rumanian rulers claim that their policies of international cooperation are in no way influenced by internal ecological and demographic factors, that they represent the interests of all inhabitants of Rumania regardless of race, religion, and nationality. In practice, however, the non-Rumanian inhabitants have little or no say in the formulation of Rumania's independent policies. The composition of the ruling Communist Party faithfully reflects the country's ethnic structure (approximately 87 per cent Rumanian); the all-powerful central organs of the Party are entirely Rumanian. The Rumanization of society and of the Party has affected the Hungarian minority less than the Jewish. The Hungarians were never influential in the higher Party echelons, but the Jews were. Ana Pauker, Iosif Chisinevski, Leonte

[12] The latest statement to that effect is Nicolae Ceausescu's of September 20, 1968, contained in *Scinteia* of September 21, 1968.

Rautu—to name just a few—had held major posts in the Party and government, and a significant part of the leading bureaucratic and technocratic cadres had been Jewish at least through 1957. The gradual downgrading and even removal of Jewish communists from positions of authority in the Party and state was due less to their association with Moscow and communist internationalism than to the resurgence of Rumanian nationalism, albeit in a socialist state. The Jews, even if Stalinists rather than Khrushchevites, could never be nationalists. The Rumanian communists' claiming of the national historic legacy, and the support of the Rumanians for the attainment of the ostensible national historic goal of a Greater Socialist Rumania, could not fail to take into account the historic anti-Hungarian and anti-Semitic tradition. Thus, Rumania is alienating her principal minority groups, Magyar and Jewish, without, however, driving them into the arms of Moscow or even Budapest or Tel Aviv. But the identification of the Hungarians and Jews with the nationalist policies of the regime is limited. They are apprehensive that the doctrine of "By ourselves" would sooner or later lead to "Great Rumanian" chauvinism, perhaps even to a Rumanian National-Socialist state. Justified as these apprehensions may be in terms of current and anticipated domestic policies, there is no evidence that the changes in the social and political order have directly affected the course of Rumania's foreign relations. The treatment of the Hungarian minority in Transylvania—a crucial source of conflict between pre-communist Hungary and Rumania—has not been renewed as an issue in contemporary relations between the two countries; and the possibility of frontier revision is not based on ill treatment so much as

on ethnic considerations and intrabloc political factors.
The revival of anti-Semitism has in no way affected
Rumanian relations with Israel and the international
Jewish community as a whole. In its official actions the
regime has protected the rights of the Jewish population and condemned anti-Semitism. The loss of political power and relegation of the Jewish bureaucratic
and intellectual cadres to subordinate positions is considered an internal affair by Jews in the rest of the
world, while the State of Israel regards the official
Rumanian position toward Israel and the rapidly ex-
panding trade relations between the two countries as
indicative of a better Rumanian order than that of the
past, and one at least tolerable for the Rumanian
Jewry.

Significant demographic factors are those generally
pertinent to agrarian societies in transition to indus-
trialism. Although the rural population has declined
from 76.6 per cent of the total in 1948 to 61.8 per cent
in 1967, the peasant-worker has not yet acquired the
skills equal to the economic requirements of the
socialist state. His acceptance of "By ourselves" may
be genuine, but he is still unable to build socialism as
rapidly and efficiently as desired by his rulers. The
relative inefficiency of the labor force has been evident
in industry; but in agriculture, too, greater efficiency
and productivity would strengthen the economic
power base of the state. These shortcomings are likely
to be overcome in time and should thus be regarded
as only temporary retarding factors in the attainment
of the goals of the regime. More pertinent factors in
the assessment of the viability of current policies are
the extent of the Rumanian people's commitment to
the aims of the regime, and the degree of their identification with communist Rumania.

Belief System

In formulating and executing national and international policies, the rulers of Rumania presuppose the existence of a popular mandate derived in part from identification of the belief system of the peoples of Rumania with that of the communist regime. The original assumptions of identification with the Communist Party and the international communist movement were gradually abandoned as unrealistic and detrimental to the attainment of the independent policies of the regime. The gradual identification of the rulers' interests and identity with those of the Rumanian people through the common bond of national historic interest has gained momentum and more than a modicum of reality since 1964. The principal element of identification between ruler and ruled in the historic context is nationalism. The nationalism emphasized by the communists is that of affection for the mother country, with a resulting commitment of all inhabitants to the development of its potential— economic, social, and cultural—to the nation's optimum capacity. Rumania, through the work of Rumanians, is to become the leading small national-socialist state in the world; the dreams of all Rumanians, past and present, will thus be realized.

This synthesis of Rumania's national and social aspirations into the new "socialist nationalism" appears to be both incomplete and unrealistic. The quintessence of historic nationalism—doubtlessly an integral part of the Rumanian belief system—was anything but socialist. The nationalist tradition was bourgeois, stressing anti-Communism, anti-Semitism, anti-Magyarism, anti-Russianism, and, above all, the Christian and Latin character of Rumanian civilization. The bourgeois nationalist legacy identified the ultimate national goal as the "embourgeoisement" of the society (primarily that of ethnic Rumanians), political control by a landlord-bourgeois oligarchy headed by a benevolent monarch, in a superficially democratic structure, and retention of the 1918 frontiers. In all probability, the national goal was a Greater Rumania for the Rumanians but not a Greater Communist Rumania.

The destruction of bourgeois nationalism and of the historic tradition connected with it was pursued with such ferocity by the Rumanian communist regime before 1960 that it outraged and alienated the vast majority of the population. The restating of the national historic legacy and the resulting search for mass identification with a socialist national interest started with recognition of the validity of the cultural components of bourgeois nationalism. The Latin characteristics of the Rumanian civilization were restored as early as 1962. Freedom of literary and artistic expression and rehabilitation of classical nationalist authors followed by 1964. As cultural contacts with France, Italy, and other Latin nations (or Western nations identified with the Latin tradition) proved politically benign, intensification of cultural relations with all Western nations gained momentum, after 1965. The strengthening of these relations, and the lessening of interbloc cultural ties, secured the adherence to the principles of the new "socialist" nationalism of pro-Western, chiefly Francophile, intellectuals, professional cadres, and students.

As the political conflict with Russia became more intense, the regime encouraged or tolerated the traditional anti-Russian sentiments of the population seeking disassociation between Rumanian communist policies and Russian. In the process of self-exoneration the Rumanian communist leadership placed the onus for its Stalinist abuses of the fifties on "foreigners" like Ana Pauker, Vasile Luca, and like-oriented Rumanian Moscovites. This line resulted in intensification of anti-Russianism and the unleashing of suppressed xenophobic, chiefly anti-Semitic, sentiments. In that respect, too, the sublimation of the main elements of bourgeois nationalism into the new nationalism became possible. The renewal of territorial claims to Bessarabia, and assertion of the integrity of the legitimate, historic boundaries of the nation, further secured the support of militant old-style nationalists for the modern version. The regime has also recognized the historic validity of the Rumanian Christian tradition—ostensibly as a cultural and historical phenomenon—and utilizes the Church and the residual religious feelings of the population as a complement to Marxism-Leninism in the creation and propagation of a Rumanian national socialist faith.

The communists' identification with the Rumanian historic tradition and the regime's derivative legitimacy have for the most part been accepted by the population, but the degree of acceptance of the "socialist" element of socialist nationalism is not clear.[13] It would be erroneous to assume that the Rumanians had been historically identified with a democratic tradition or had entertained democratic aspirations. Authoritarianism had been the rule, not the exception. Modern dictatorships like Marshal Antonescu's received more

[13] The extent of mass acceptance of the new nationalism was demonstrated during the Czechoslovak crisis of August, 1968, when spontaneous pro-Ceausescu (and anti-Russian) manifestations occurred throughout Rumania. See *Scinteia,* particularly the issues published between August 23 and 31, 1968.

than passing popular approval. Nevertheless, at least since the emancipation of the peasantry in 1864, all regimes had paid at least lip service to the principles of democracy and of respect for individual property rights. The rigidity of the communist police state before 1958 was to a considerable extent a reaction to mass dissatisfaction with the violation of individual property rights. It was the peasants' opposition to agricultural collectivization, and the destruction of the traditional spiritual and material bases of the village which followed, that scared the communists—at least as much as the disaffection of the intellectuals and of the former propertied classes. The continuing rigidity, even after the need for popular support for an anti-Russian course became evident, was largely the result of continuing political insecurity because of mass disaffection.

The encouragement of traditional nationalism, with all its implications, doubtlessly conditioned the reaction of the masses to the communist regime, making them more receptive to a *modus vivendi*. The regime's economic concessions—such as increases in wages and farm subsidies, restoration of private property rights to the extent of granting the population the right to acquire private residences and engage in certain private commercial activities, and, above all, the steadily greater allocation of funds for the production and distribution of consumer goods—have increased the domestic support for Ceausescu's Rumania. However, not until 1967, and particularly since the Budapest conference of February, 1968, did the regime move in the direction of recognizing individual rights and abandoning its dogmatic positions. The doctrine of democratic socialism, implying popular commitment to "socialist nationalism," was enunciated explicitly only in December, 1967.[14] Then, at the National Conference of the Rumanian Communist Party, Ceausescu made a formal commitment to liberalization and decentralization of governmental and party activities and controls.

Nevertheless, despite planned economic and administrative reorganization of the country to coincide with the continuing decentralization of economic and industrial activities away from Bucharest, the ultimate direction of all economic and political activities rests with the Party. Experimentation and decentralization comparable to Yugoslavia's or even to Hungary's are not likely in the foreseeable future. Nor are innovations contemplated in altering the role of the Party in governmental and cultural affairs. The explicit condemnation of Stalinism and of Gheorghiu-Dej's Stalinist practices of earlier years contained in the Party's decision of April, 1968, to rehabilitate victims of Stalinist oppression promised no reforms comparable to those carried out in contemporary Czechoslovakia. The Party remains the ultimate source of power and the ever-present director of all activities of the population. Liberalization is possible only through the Party, and ultimately through Nicolae Ceausescu who, symbolically, assumed the dual role of head of the Party and of the state in December, 1967.

The nation's response to this limited liberalization has been positive, but it has not overcome the spirit of passive opposition, if not outright resistance, of a substantial segment of the collectivized peasantry to the agricultural policies of the regime. This opposition is likely to diminish as further economic concessions are

[14] On this point consult the fundamental article, "Socialist Democracy—Source of Power and Dynamism in Our Order," *Scinteia,* March 14, 1968.

made. However, nothing short of decollectivization would fully placate the rural population. Pockets of discontent are found also among intellectuals and professional cadres dissatisfied with inadequate housing and salaries and continuing restrictions on freedom of travel abroad. Nevertheless, the regime's foreign policies are endorsed, often with enthusiasm, by the vast majority of the population. The success and viability of those policies, as they affect integration and community building, will not be affected by lack of popular support; rather, success will be determined by economic and external political factors.

Rumania as a Self-fulfilling Unit

Rumania's ability to attain the planned economic goals with her own resources was carefully scrutinized in the 1964 statement; the conclusion justified the autarchic policies advocated by the regime, in that the country's natural resources are basically adequate. However, the same analysis revealed that integration under COMECON would not serve Rumania's aims insofar as her resources would be used for developing the economies of only certain members of that organization in a manner detrimental to the national interest. Such integration would not be based on the principle of mutual advantage, and it would jeopardize the completion of socialist construction in Rumania because of the imposition of external economic policies on the national economy. By contrast, the fullest utilization of Rumania's natural and manpower resources in collaboration with non-bloc nations would bring about the most expeditious and advantageous development of the country's economy, as well as the most effective and rapid attainment of the national goal.

The experience since 1964 has largely corroborated these basic assumptions. The annual average growth rate in industry has been quite spectacular, exceeding 20 per cent in the chemical and electric power industries, 15 per cent in machine building, metal working, and nonferrous metallurgy, 12 per cent in ferrous metallurgy and light industry, and somewhat lower percentages in other spheres of industrial development. Agricultural production has also increased considerably; the growth rate has been 7.5 per cent per annum.[15] Rumania's economic dependence on the Soviet bloc, however, has not decreased at a comparable rate. Even though her foreign trade with the West, most notably with Germany, France, Italy, and the United States, has nearly doubled since 1964, that with the Soviet Union alone is still nearly twice as large as with those four countries combined.[16]

Altogether, the member nations of COMECON could strangle the Rumanian economy should concerted economic pressures be contemplated by the Soviet Union, while Russian economic pressures alone could paralyze certain areas of industrial development. In fact, Russia's slowing down of deliveries of industrial equipment and raw materials, for ostensibly economic reasons, has reportedly created minor economic crises since 1967, and could conceivably retard the attainment of the country's ambitious plans for economic development. Even if in 1968 the possibility of Russia's delivering a paralyzing economic blow is still remote, the Rumanian leaders are fearful of Soviet

[15] Consult Montias, *Economic Development,* pp. 1 ff.
[16] *Ibid.,* pp. 135 ff.

retaliation. Self-sufficiency is an illusion in terms of current Rumanian plans for economic development, and it is recognized as such by Rumanian economic planners. Despite the continuing emphasis on independence, interdependence is gradually being accepted as a fact of economic life. Relations with COMECON are being normalized on the bases of mutual advantage and respect for the rights of individual members, although the search for alternatives continues unabated. The Rumanians would prefer economic independence from the Soviet bloc, but such seems hardly attainable at the current juncture in international economic affairs. Thus, in 1968, the Rumanian formulas for economic integration within the bloc and development of extra-bloc relations entail serious risks despite their essential success.

Consensus on Present and Future Integration

In the last analysis, the determination of Rumania's leaders to attain the national goal "By ourselves" and with partners of their choice—in other words, through voluntary and mutually advantageous association with sovereign states (and friendly communist parties)—is dependent upon the vicissitudes of international political relations. The possibility of forcible termination of the independent course and reintegration of Rumania into the Soviet bloc by Russian military or economic action can by no means be excluded after the Soviet intervention in Czechoslovakia. Reassertion of Soviet domination over a smaller socialist camp, with corresponding strengthening of the Soviet position in Eastern Europe, has in fact become probable. The Rumanians are painfully aware of these potential dangers to the maintenance of their independence and are trying to appease the Soviet Union without, however, sacrificing the basic tenets of their political and socioeconomic philosophies.[17] The essential question, in the fall of 1968, is whether Ceausescu's Rumania will be able to avoid the fate of Czechoslovakia and maintain its status as a sovereign communist nation state.

The basic factor in evaluating the current, and prognosticating the future, Rumanian policies toward integration and community building remains that of irreconcilability of the fundamental political conflict with the Soviet Union. A meaningful reconciliation appears unlikely so long as the present Rumanian and Russian ruling élites remain in power. So long as that situation persists, anything but *pro forma* reintegration of Rumania into the Soviet bloc is excluded. This is not to say that integration would be detrimental to Rumania were it possible to achieve it under terms safeguarding the Rumanian Party's vital political interests. In the absence of such safeguards, Rumania's "independent course" is likely to be pursued, albeit with greater caution and finesse. Should Ceausescu be able to walk the tight-rope successfully, his regime would be assured of ever greater popular support; his "socialist nationalist" goals may, however, prove elusive.

[17] The repeated Rumanian assurances given to the Soviet Union and her conservative partners by Ceausescu on Rumania's loyalty to the cause of socialism and commitments to the Warsaw Pact and COMECON did not imply renunciation of Rumania's commitment to the maintenance of advantageous relations with all nations, including West Germany, and protection—by force of arms if necessary—of the country's independence. All of Ceausescu's speeches—contained in *Scinteia* almost daily since August 22, 1968—are unequivocal in that respect.

SELECTED BIBLIOGRAPHY

Cretzianu, Alexandre, ed. *Captive Rumania: A Decade of Soviet Rule.* New York: Praeger, 1956.

Fischer-Galati, Stephen, ed. *Romania.* New York: Praeger, 1957.

Fischer-Galati, Stephen. *The New Rumania: From People's Democracy to Socialist Republic.* Cambridge, Mass.: The M.I.T. Press, 1967.

Ionescu, Ghita. *Communism in Rumania 1944–1962.* London: Oxford University Press, 1964.

Montias, John Michael. *Economic Development in Communist Rumania.* Cambridge, Mass.: The M.I.T. Press, 1967.

Patrascanu, Lucretiu D. *Sous trois dictatures.* Paris: Vitiano, 1946.

Roberts, Henry L. *Rumania: Political Problems of an Agrarian State.* New Haven: Yale University Press, 1951.

Roucek, Joseph S. *Contemporary Roumania and Her Problems: A Study in Modern Nationalism.* Stanford: Stanford University Press, 1932.

Seton-Watson, R. W. *A History of the Roumanians: From Roman Times to the Completion of Unity.* Cambridge: Cambridge University Press, 1934.

DATE DUE